LOCKE

PHILOSOPHERS IN CONTEXT

General Editor:

Stephan Körner
Professor of Philosophy
Yale University

PHILOSOPHERS·IN·CONTEXT

LOCKE

R. S. Woolhouse

Senior Lecturer in Philosophy,
University of York

University of Minnesota Press · Minneapolis

Published by the University of Minnesota Press,
2037 University Avenue Southeast, Minneapolis MN 55414

Second printing 1984

Printed in Great Britain

ISBN 0-8166-1249-8
     0-8166-1389-3 (pbk)

To Jan

Contents

Preface

References in what follows, if not self-explanatory, have the form '*Descartes* (1) 2.32' – a reference to page 32 of the second volume of the first work of Descartes listed in the 'Bibliography of Books and Articles referred to more than once'. I am grateful to Stephen Körner, the editor of this series, and to Gerd Buchdahl for suggesting I might write this book; to Susan Mendus and Ian Tipton for their very helpful comments on its penultimate draft; and to Susan Mendus for her help with its proofreading.

CHAPTER 1

1 Introduction

John Locke was born in Somerset in 1632 during the reign of
Charles I, and died in Essex in 1704 at the beginning of Queen
Anne's. Spinoza, Vermeer, and Wren also were born in 1632;
and Locke's life overlapped those of Hobbes (1588-1679), Descartes (1596-1650), and Leibniz (1646-1716); of Galileo (1564-
1642), Harvey (1578-1657), Boyle (1627-91), and Newton
(1642-1727); of Purcell (1658-95), Handel (1685-1759), and
Bach (1685-1750); of Rubens (1577-1640) and of Rembrandt
(1606-69); and of Milton (1608-74), Molière (1622-73), Pepys
(1633-1703), Defoe (1661-1731), and Swift (1667-1745). The
dates of the first barometer (1642), the Civil War (1642-51), the
making of violins by Stradivari (1641-1737), the Restoration
(1660), the plague and fire of London (1666), the founding of
the Royal Society (1662) and of Greenwich Observatory (1675)
all fell within his life.

In 1647 his father, a lawyer and stern Puritan Parliamen-
tarian, sent him to Westminster School, near where Charles I
was executed in 1649. He went on in 1652 to Christ Church,
Oxford, where he first studied logic, grammar, rhetoric, Greek,
and moral philosophy; going on later to other subjects such as
history and Hebrew. He was elected in 1658 to a Senior Studentship, tenable for life, and lectured on Greek and rhetoric.
He was attracted to the study of medicine, eventually taking his
M.B. degree in 1674.

In 1666, acting in an as-yet formally unqualified medical
capacity, Locke met Lord Ashley, later Earl of Shaftesbury. He
entered into his service, initially solely as a medical adviser but
increasingly – particularly after 1672 when Ashley became
Lord Chancellor – as a political secretary and adviser.

In 1675 ill-health took him to France where he spent four years in travel and study. On his return to England in 1679 he re-entered the service of Shaftesbury who became engaged against the Catholic King, Charles II, to establish the Protestant Duke of Monmouth as the successor to the throne. In 1682 Shaftesbury, who had already once been charged with, but acquitted of, high treason, retreated to Holland where he died the next year.

In that year, 1683, Locke too went to Holland, where he was when King Charles forced the Christ Church authorities to deprive him of his Studentship. Charles died in 1685 and the accession of his brother James was followed by Monmouth's unsuccessful rebellion. Locke was cited as a Monmouth supporter and the ensuing application for his extradition from Holland forced him to live for a while under the assumed name of Dr van der Linden.

By 1686 political suspicion of him appeared to have lapsed but he remained in Holland where he was able to devote time to scholarly activities. His time there ended in 1689 when, shortly after the events of the 'glorious revolution' (the flight of James II and the accession to the throne of William of Orange), he returned to England.

Here he declined William's offer of ambassadorial posts, accepting instead appointment as Commissioner of Appeals. In 1691 he went to live in Essex at Oates, the house of Sir Francis and Lady Damaris Masham, where he stayed as one of the family till his death on 28 October 1704. Throughout his life he had had recurrent bouts of asthma and bronchitis, but despite increasingly declining health these years were spent productively in yet more scholarly activity and also (1696-1700) as a Commissioner of the Board of Trade and Plantations.[1]

Locke was known and active in public affairs. He nevertheless found time to write and publish on a considerable variety of topics – not only on various branches of philosophy, but also on education, economics, theology, and medicine. The last (a nineteenth-century) edition of his work was in ten volumes; and since 1975 there has been appearing what will be, in some thirty volumes (including eight of correspondence), a complete edition of his writings (both published and unpublished). His fame rests mainly on *An Essay Concerning Human Understanding* (1690) and *Two Treatises of Government*(1690). But his *Letters Concerning Toleration* (1689-92), *Some Thoughts Concerning Education* (1693), and *The Reasonableness of Christianity* (1695) are by no means insignificant. We will be concerned here solely with what has always been judged to be easily the most important of these works, the *Essay*. So we will consider only what might broadly be termed Locke's theory of knowledge. We will not touch on his political theory, the other area for which he is well known.[2]

Locke began work on *An Essay Concerning Human Understanding* in London, about twenty years before its eventual publication, during his first period of service with Shaftesbury. Two manuscripts survive from this beginning, both dated 1671.[3] At any rate the first two of the four books into which the *Essay* is divided had reached something very like their final shape in 1685, in a manuscript which was begun a couple of years earlier soon after Locke's arrival in Holland at the beginning of his second period there. By the end of 1686 there seems to have been a complete manuscript.[4] Locke published a lengthy abstract or summary of the *Essay* in France in 1688.[5] But the *Essay* itself was worked over for a year or so until his return to England in 1689. At the end of this year, though it bore the date '1690', it was on sale.

It made an immediate impression and has continued to be read. There was a second edition, containing some substantial changes, in 1694, a third in 1695, an enlarged fourth in 1700, and a fifth, which Locke had worked on before he died, in 1706. It was translated into French in 1700 (with many later editions) and into Latin in 1701. Either by itself or in collections of Locke's work it had over two dozen English editions in the eighteenth century, over one dozen in the nineteenth, and about half a dozen in the twentieth as well as reprints of influential nineteenth-century editions. Particularly in the nineteenth century it was 'abridged', 'analysed in question and answer form', 'catechised', 'epitomized', 'issued with questions for examination', 'selected from', and 'summarised'. The immediate effect of the *Essay* showed itself also in the amount of contemporary discusion and criticism it excited [see *Yolton* (1)].

The *Essay* is currently and easily available in a number of versions, both abridged and unabridged. Both for the serious scholar and for all but the most casual reader the best is that done by P.H.Nidditch for the Clarendon edition of the *Works of John Locke*.[6] This is available relatively cheaply in paperback.

Though some of these editions help a little by modernising the spelling, Locke's *Essay* is bound to present initial difficulties of understanding, particularly to anyone unused to reading outside of the twentieth or nineteenth century. To begin with, there are unfamiliar sentence constructions, vocabulary and punctuation. Furthermore each page of an edition which, like Nidditch's, is faithful to the original, presents an apparent jumble of capital letters and italics. But behind the appearance there are some general rules, and things begin to fall into place as one becomes aware of them. Nouns have capital initial letters wherever they occur in a sentence, and the word 'idea' is always in italics. Then, most usefully and importantly, other words in italics, scattered as they may be, are intended to be read together to form a sentence which summarises the section in which they appear. It is often necessary, as Locke advises his readers, that 'a little allowance be made for the Grammatical Construction'. But this nice idea works quite well. Locke's personal style, too, is something that has to be contended with. He has a bad reputation for being clumsy, laboured, and repetitive; and it is true that his sentences do not always carry one along in a smoothly flowing manner. Nevertheless he often rewards his readers with stylish passages of great elegance, with memorable epigrams, and not infrequently with pungent humour and dry wit.

A final difficulty even when one is used to the words and sentences on the page is that the ideas they are meant to convey are not readily comprehensible. They may, along with their mode of presentation, be unsympathetically dismissed as just unintelligible and not worth consideration. In fact Locke is far less open to such criticism than are some of his contemporaries, particularly those of an older tradition that he attacked. When he is read alongside them he comes over as refreshingly intelligible, 'modern', and full of life and vigour. In an appraisal of Locke's contribution to the history of thought Gilbert Ryle remarks that the *Essay* is a watershed. 'The intellectual atmosphere since Locke has had quite a different smell from what it had before Locke. If we could fly back in a time-rocket to England in 1700, we could already breathe its air, and we could already converse with our new acquaintances there without being lost. In the England of, say, 1660, we should gasp like fishes out of water' [147]. But despite the fact that the *Essay* celebrates new beginnings rather than commemorates a dying past its ideas do need explanation and commentary. Sometimes they need this precisely because they are an attack on earlier and even more unfamiliar thought and ideas.

Locke tends not to identify his targets by name. This hides the extent to which there is a background to the arguments and ideas of the *Essay* and the frequency with which it makes allusions to and presupposes acquaintance with Locke's intellectual predecessors and contemporaries. The vague reference to 'those who tell us' [III. iv. 10] may not appear to be to anyone in particular. However in an early version of this passage we find an explicit reference to 'the Cartesians' [(2) 132], followers of the French philosopher Descartes.[7] Similarly the insignificant and passing reference in 'The Epistle to the Reader' to 'Cursory Readers' is in fact a reference to John Norris, an early critic of the *Essay*.[8] Many of these allusions, presuppositions, and background ideas would have been familiar to the educated reader of the *Essay* when it appeared. So, of course, would the significance and import of what Locke was saying. But it is now nearly three hundred years since the *Essay* appeared, so one aim of this book is to point to and explain some of Locke's main themes and to reveal and make explicit something of the context in which they were formulated and made public. I shall also, both along the way and in the final section, say something about the present significance of the *Essay*.

Notes

[1] Though the interpretation of some events in Locke's life is not completely settled, the authoritative biography is Maurice Cranston, *John Locke: A Biography* (Longmans, London and New York, 1957).

[2] The best edition of and introduction to Locke's *Two Treatises of Government* is P. Laslett's (Cambridge University Press, Cambridge, 1960).

[3] They are known as draft A [(1)] and draft B [(2)].

⁴ This is known as draft C (partly printed in *Aaron*).

⁵ In English in *Locke* (4) 365-99.

⁶ Oxford, 1975. All *Essay* quotations, often with omitted italics, are from this edition. Except occasionally when identified by page number they are identified by book, chapter, and section (e.g. I.ii.1). Unless otherwise stated all Locke quotations are from the *Essay*.

⁷ René Descartes (1596-1650) is often described as 'the father of modern philosophy'. His *Rules for the Direction of the Mind* (1628), *Meditations on the First Philosophy* (1641), and *Principles of Philosophy* (1644) were very influential in the seventeenth century and afterwards. Though, as we shall see, Locke disagreed with Descartes on many matters, Lady Masham reported that 'the first books, as Mr. Locke himself has told me, which gave him a relish of philosophical things, were those of Descartes' [quoted in *Fox Bourne* 1.61-2].

⁸ Norris (1657-1711), an English clergyman and disciple of the French Cartesian Nicolas Malebranche (1638-1715) was the first in print to criticise the *Essay*, in his *Reflections upon a late Essay concerning the Human Understanding* (1690). Locke and Norris fell out in 1692 about the opening of a letter for Locke, which Lady Masham had entrusted to Norris. In 1693 Locke wrote, partially in reply to Norris's criticisms, *Remarks upon Some of Mr. Norris' Books wherein he asserts P. Malebranche's opinion of our seeing all things in God.*

2 Origins and Aims of the Essay

In 'The Epistle to the Reader' [7] Locke himself tells us how he came to set about writing the *Essay*. He and some friends had met with problems in their discussion of 'a Subject very remote from this'. It occurred to him that the way through might be first to 'examine our own Abilities, and see, what Objects our Understandings were, or were not fitted to deal with'. They agreed to try this; and it was Locke's own 'hasty and undigested Thoughts . . . which I set down against our next Meeting' which were the beginnings of what twenty years later was the final *Essay*. Of course these first thoughts were expanded and refined over those years, but their purpose and direction did not change. The introduction to the completed work still announces the aim as being to 'enquire into the Original, Certainty, and Extent of humane Knowledge; together, with the Grounds and Degrees of Belief, Opinion, and Assent' [I.i.2].

As Locke says, the subject which started the thing off was 'remote from this'. But it may be helpful to know just what those 'five or six Friends meeting at my Chamber' were initially discussing. When the *Essay* came to be published Locke presented copies of it to friends. One of these, James Tyrrell,[1] wrote in the margin of his copy (which survives today in the British Museum) that the meeting 'was in winter 1673 as I remember being myself one of those that met there when the discourse began about the Principles of morality and reveal'd Religion'. Tyrrell, looking back from 1690, is slightly mistaken about the date. The meeting must have been two or three years earlier than 1673 for both drafts A and B of the *Essay* are dated '1671'. It is a pity that draft A is rather too long for a discussion paper. It would have been nice to think that it is nothing less than those very first 'hasty and undigested Thoughts' which Locke set down for the next meeting with his friends.[2]

What questions might the group have been asking about the

'Principles of morality and reveal'd Religion'? It is plausible to think that Locke and his friends were discussing topics such as the manner in which the principles of morality are discovered and known to be true, and such as the role of revelation as a source and foundation of morality and religion. If they were discussing these questions about knowledge in these particular areas it would explain why they eventually felt the need to have some wider understanding of how and to what extent man can acquire knowledge of any sort. Questions about whether it is possible for us to have religious and moral knowledge could easily lead to the question what 'Objects' in general 'our Understandings were, or were not fitted to deal with'.

Locke's final concern with knowledge in general and his possible initial concern with religious and moral knowledge in particular, help us to place the *Essay* in a wider historical context. In order to do this we need to begin by noting a certain respect in which his so-far announced aims and intentions look beyond themselves and are means to a further end. On the second occasion when he refers to what 'gave the first Rise' to the *Essay* and to his plan 'to take a Survey of our own Understandings, examine our own Powers, and see to what Things they were adapted', he reveals a further desire or aim. This is the desire to rescue people from a despair caused by scepticism about the amount of knowledge we have. He evidently envisages that his enquiry into the extent of our understanding and intellectual ability will effect this rescue:

> Men, extending their Enquiries beyond their Capacities ... 'tis no Wonder, that they raise Questions, and multiply Disputes, which never coming to any clear Resolution, are proper only to continue and increase their Doubts, and to confirm them at last in perfect Scepticism. Whereas were the Capacities of our Understandings well considered, the Extent of our Knowledge once discovered, and the Horizon found ... between what is, and what is not comprehensible by us, Men would perhaps with less scruple acquiesce in the avow'd Ignorance of the one, and imploy their Thoughts and Discourse, with more Advantage and Satisfaction in the other. [I.i.7; also 2]

Since Locke hopes that his enquiries into the extent of human knowledge will be a remedy for scepticism one might expect that the results of these enquiries would themselves be completely non-sceptical. The above quotation indicates, however, that this would be a mistake. Locke's final position is not that of thinking there is no basis for scepticism. He does not think that his conclusions and results show that man can recognise the truth on all matters and does have unlimited means to acquire knowledge. Surprising as it may seem, Locke's own final view has an element of scepticism about it. He does not deny that the truth often outstrips our ability to know it. On the contrary he says that 'the Comprehension of our Understandings, comes exceeding short of the vast Extent of Things'; our knowledge falls short 'of an universal, or perfect Comprehension of whatsoever is' [I.i.5]. But if his own conclusions are to any degree sceptical, if he does not oppose scepticism by showing that there are no limits to our knowledge and intellectual abilities, how can he hope to deal with sceptical despair? The answer lies in the nature of his scepticism which is both *limited* and *constructive*. These two features explain how, beginning from a basically sceptical position, he can still hope to avoid the worrying, doubting outlook which often characterises such a position. What exactly are these features and how do they have this effect?

To begin with, Locke's scepticism is not perfectly general. He thinks that there are *some* things which we can know and fully understand. His examination of the human understanding is intended to show this. He hopes, once it has been shown, that people will gain confidence and be freed from the despair engendered by the belief that we can know and understand nothing. An awareness of what we have and can get will relieve our worry about what lies beyond our reach. '[W]hen we have well survey'd the Powers of our own Minds, and made some Estimate what we may expect from them, we shall not be inclined . . . to . . . Despair of knowing any thing . . . and disclaim all Knowledge, because some Things are not to be understood' [I.i.6].

Of course even though there are things we can know and understand, other things still lie beyond knowledge. Why may we not fall into despair about them? Locke argues for a more balanced attitude here. He hopes to show that there are things that we should not *expect* to know; and he believes that showing

this will, as before, result in our being undespairingly content
with our ignorance or lack of knowledge:

> If by this Enquiry into the Nature of the Understanding, I can discover the
> Powers thereof; how far they reach . . . I suppose it may be of use, to prevail
> with the busy Mind of Man, to be more cautious in meddling with things
> exceeding its Comprehension; . . . to sit down in a quiet Ignorance of those
> Things, which, upon Examination, are found to be beyond the reach of our
> Capacities. . . . If we can find out, how far the Understanding can extend
> its view . . . we may learn to content our selves with what is attainable by us
> in this State.[I.i.4; also 6]

Locke is not clearly right to think that showing that there are
things we should not expect to know because our capacities are
limited will result in our being quietly content with our ignorance. It is not clear that the recognition of our own limitations will necessarily have the effect which he intends. The
reaction of some may well be to 'boldly quarrel with their own
Constitution, and throw away the Blessings their Hands are
fill'd with, because they are not big enough to grasp every thing'
[I.i.5].

The second feature of Locke's scepticism that some things lie
beyond our understanding is its constructiveness. He suggests
that what we *do* know tends to be what we *need* to know to deal
with what is important and crucial to us. For instance we *do*
know, he believes, our duties and obligations to each other and
to God. Moreover at least many of the things we cannot know
are, nevertheless, things about which we can have beliefs sufficiently well-founded to enable us to deal with the practicalities
and problems of everyday life. This idea that our faculties and
understandings, limited as they may be, are sufficient for our
needs is fundamental to Locke's thinking and attitudes. He
often expresses it:

> Men have Reason to be well satisfied with what God hath thought fit for
> them, since he has given them . . . Whatsoever is necessary for the Con-
> veniences of Life, and Information of Vertue; and has put within the reach
> of their Discovery the comfortable Provision for this Life and the Way that
> leads to a better. How short soever their Knowledge may come of an
> universal, or perfect Comprehension of whatsoever is, it yet secures their
> great Concernments. [I.i.5; also 6, (4) 86 ff.]

So far we have observed two things about Locke's explicitly announced aim in the *Essay* of tracing how and to what extent we have knowledge. First, it may reasonably be supposed that the aim originated in specific questions about how the principles of morality are discovered and known to be true, and about what role relevation has as a source and foundation of morality and religion. Second, though his delineation of the boundaries of knowledge is basically sceptical it is both a limited and a constructive scepticism. It is because of this that he hopes to avoid or defeat the despair which characteristically results from the straightforwardly sceptical idea that 'either there is no such thing as Truth at all; or that Mankind hath no sufficient Means to attain a certain Knowledge of it' [I.i.2].

Now Locke's interest in the question of what we can or cannot know (whether in general, or specifically on matters of morality and religion) and the limited, constructive nature of his sceptical answer to it, gives him a place in a tradition of discussion and intellectual debate which stretches back well beyond the beginning of the seventeenth century. A brief survey of this tradition will show us that the questions Locke raised were not raised by him out of the blue.[3] It was not out of some idiosyncratic and purely personal interest that he discussed them. He was a child of his time.

A convenient point to begin is France in the 1560s. There appeared then the first printed editions of the work of Sextus Empiricus, an Hellenic writer of about 200 A.D. Sextus is the main source for our knowledge of the history of Greek Scepticism or Pyrrhonism, a history which began with Pyrrho of Elis (360?-275? B.C.) and ended with Sextus himself. In Sextus' work we find an account and defence of Scepticism together with a corresponding attack on Dogmatism.[4] The upshot of Scepticism, as Sextus defines it, is a suspension of judgement rather than a dogmatic denial that there is truth or that if there is we do not know it. He outlines ten *tropes, modes*, or ways which lead to this suspense. The fourth and the fifth, for examples, suggest that though we can certainly say how temperatures and shapes appear differently to different people or from different positions we can say nothing of their 'nature', of how they really are. For 'the vestibule of the bath-house, which warms those entering from outside, chills those coming out of the bath-house if they stop long in it' [65]. Similarly, 'the same tower from a distance appears round but from a near point quadrangular' [71]. So we should suspend judgement on such matters as temperatures and shapes.

An important feature of Sextus' attack on the Dogmatic idea that we can know the realities of things in their 'natures', that we can know the truth about things as they really are, is his discussion of what is called the 'criterion of truth'. What is the criterion 'which the Dogmatists employ for the judging of truth' [161]? They believe that truth can be discovered. How then is it found? What is the basis on which what is true may be distinguished from what is not? Sextus argues that in fact the Dogmatist who believes that truth can be found needs to provide three different criteria. First there is the question of the *agent*, the criterion 'by whom' truth is discovered or judged. Then there is the question of the *instrument*, the criterion 'by means of which' the agent discovers or judges of the truth. Third, there is the question of the *procedure*, the criterion 'according to which' the judgement is made.[5]

Sextus concludes that he can find no satisfactory answer to any of these questions. Even if it is allowed that *man* is the proper agent to discover or judge the truth it cannot be decided which man or men should have their judgement accepted. As to the 'instrument' that would be used, this could only be either the senses or the intellect, or both. But the senses are unreliable, they 'contradict themselves, and their dispute is incapable of decision' [187]; and one man's intellect will decide one thing and another's another. Finally, man cannot by his intellect use his sensory presentations as the procedure 'according to which' he judges about external reality. 'For how is the intellect to know whether the affections of the senses are similar to the objects of sense when it has not itself encountered the external objects?'[199]. Sextus will naturally not be dogmatic about whether or not there is such a thing as truth, but he concludes that even if there is, there is, in no sense, any 'criterion' of it.

The rediscovery in the sixteenth century of these ideas of Sextus added fuel and gave new forms of expression to one of the main controversies of the Reformation which Martin Luther

(1483?-1546) had precipitated some thirty years earlier. This was the controversy about the 'rule of faith'. According to the Catholic Church, the sources of religious knowledge, the tests of what was or was not true in religion, were Church tradition, Papal decrees, and Church Councils. Luther, however, had broken with the Catholic Church in holding that neither the Pope nor Council was infallible. The test and source of religious truth and knowledge was not the word of the Church or its leaders. Rather it was the Scriptures as understood by a faithful and sincere reader.

The question of the 'rule of faith', 'What is the source and touch-stone for religious knowledge and belief?', is obviously a special case of Sextus' general question about the criterion of truth as such. Thus, for example, the aim of Gentian Hervet, one of the early French editors of Sextus' work, was that the Pyrrhonist arguments should, by showing that the matter could not be decided, defuse and undermine the disputes about religious authority. This would leave the way open for the acceptance of Catholicism on the basis of faith. Discussion of the rediscovered sceptical arguments concerning the 'criterion' of truth continued to cross-fertilise and interact with the theological disagreements of the Reformation into the seventeenth century. By Locke's time and particularly in a Protestant context the position had begun to change. The rival criteria for religious truth were not the Scriptures and the Church, but rather the Scriptures and man's reason. The detail of Locke's own position with regard to religious knowledge and the 'rule of faith' will be looked at later, in section 15.

In the sixteenth and seventeenth centuries the ideas generated by exposure to Sextus' scepticism informed discussion of sorts of knowledge other than religious, for example, knowledge of the natural world. From the vantage point of 1701, at the end of the century with which we are mainly concerned, John Norris remarked in a discussion of non-religious knowledge that the '*Criterium of Truth* [has been] so much talk'd of both by the old and new Philosophers' [2.167]. Thus, throughout the period there were various reactions to the sceptical arguments that whether or not there is such a thing as truth there is no 'criterion' of it and hence knowledge is impossible. One kind of reaction was that of writers such as Francis Bacon and Lord Herbert of Cherbury who, in their different ways, suggested that with proper care and caution knowledge of the natural world *is* attainable.[6] Another was that of Pierre Gassendi and his older friend Marin Mersenne who aimed to find a middle course between dogmatism and scepticism. They suggested that though we cannot go beyond appearances and sense-presentations nevertheless reason and experience can enable us to produce explanations and expectations about how and under what conditions our experiences will shift and vary.[7] Yet another reaction, not completely different from Gassendi's, formed the basis of a tradition of constructive scepticism which has been traced in seventeenth-century England, both in religious and non-religious areas. This allows that in many areas absolute certainty is not to be had. But it insists that we can nevertheless attain beliefs sufficiently certain for our needs. This train of thought can be found in writers such as Robert Boyle, Joseph Glanvill, and others associated with the Royal Society.[8] From what we saw earlier in outline of his views about the extent of knowledge it is plain that Locke belongs to this tradition of constructive scepticism. We must now turn to the detail of what he says.

Notes

[1] James Tyrrell (1642-1718) met Locke at Oxford and became a good and lifelong friend. He wrote on historical and political matters.

[2] There is some earlier manuscript material which may be part of those very first thoughts; see Peter Laslett, 'Locke and the First Earl of Shaftesbury', *Mind*, 61 (1952).

[3] This brief survey is based on *Popkin*.

[4] See *Sextus Empiricus*, vol. 1, trans. R. G. Bury (Heinemann, London, 1933).

[5] 'Procedure' is not Sextus' term but was used in seventeenth-century discussions of scepticism. In these discussions the instrument was called the criterion 'id per quod', the procedure the criterion 'id secundum quod'; see *The Selected Works of Pierre Gassendi*, ed. and trans. C. B. Brush (Johnson, New York and London, 1972).

[6] This reaction is discussed in *Van Leeuwen*, ch. 1 (Bacon) and *Popkin*, ch.8 (Herbert). For information about Bacon see section 4 below. Edward Herbert, first Baron of Cherbury (1583-1648) is known as the father of

English deism and wrote on historical, religious, and metaphysical matters as in his *De Veritate* (Paris, 1624).

7 This reaction is discussed in *Popkin*, ch.7. Marin Mersenne (1588-1648) was a French mathematician, philosopher, and scientist who was very influential in his century. His defence against scepticism is in his *La Verité des Sciences* (1625). Pierre Gassendi (1592-1655) was responsible for the revival of ancient atomism (see section 12 below). He too was influential in his time and would be more discussed now were his works available in English.

8 *Van Leeuwen*, passim. For information on Robert Boyle and the Royal Society see section 4 below. Joseph Glanvill (1636-80) wrote a number of books on religious and philosophical matters, the most famous of which is *The Vanity of Dogmatizing* (1661). Very much one of the 'moderns' discussed in section 4 he was a vigorous defender of the Royal Society, to which he was elected in 1664.

3 Innatism attacked

After its initial chapter of Introduction the *Essay* divides into two distinct parts of quite unequal length. First there is the rest of Book I, 'Of Innate Notions', which is devoted to the criticism and rejection of certain views about 'the Original, Certainty, and Extent of humane Knowledge' which Locke found held at the time. Then there are Books II, III, and IV which are generally constructive and present Locke's own views.

One positive thesis which is developed and argued for in the second of these parts is that 'all our Knowledge is founded [in experience]; and from that it ultimately derives it self' [II.i.2]. It may not be so clear till later that this thesis has consequences for the 'certainty and extent' of our knowledge. It is immediately obvious however that it has consequences for the 'original' of knowledge, i.e. for where knowledge originates. It is important to see exactly what these are, for we will not properly understand Book I, the negative and destructive part of the *Essay*, unless we do.

Locke says that Knowledge is 'ultimately' derived from experience, not that it 'immediately' is. What experience directly provides is not knowledge itself, but rather its 'materials' [II.i.25]. This distinction between *knowledge* and the *materials of knowledge* is Locke's own. It is embodied in the answer to an objection which he reports was made to him early on [(1) 67-8]. Can it really be, he was asked, that all our knowledge is derived from experience? Surely there are some truths of which we are certain but which we could not have learnt 'from our senses'? We know, for example, that 'it is the property of all numbers to be even or od. But we can by noe means be assured by our senses that this property belongs to all numbers because neither our senses nor thoughts have been conversant about all numbers'. Locke's response to this objection is simply to clarify matters and to make a distinction. He is *not* claiming, he says, that all knowledge, 'was to be made out to us by our senses for this was to leave noe room for reason at all, which I thinke by a right traceing of those Ideas which it hath received from Sense or Sensation may come to . . . knowledge . . . which our senses could never have discoverd'. His claim is rather, he says, that we have in our minds no *ideas* not derived from experience. His thesis is not that our realisation and *knowledge* that all numbers are even or odd depends on experience. It is that the 'Ideas of that proposition' are experience-dependent. The *idea* of an odd number, for example, is such as 'a schooleboy may learne from dividing his cherry stones'. But our *knowledge* of the proposition does not directly derive from our senses. In a way we shall examine later, it is dependent also on reason.

Now Book I consists of an attack on a doctrine of innateness. Does it attack one which holds that *knowledge* does not come from experience but is innate; or does it attack one which holds that the materials of knowledge, *ideas*, are innate? Of course Locke could hardly agree with a doctrine of either sort, for if there were innate knowledge the ideas in which it is expressed would be innate too. It is possible, moreover, that doctrines of innateness were sometimes indifferently about both ideas and knowledge. As will become clear, however, it is important that we persist in asking, Against which of the two, innate *ideas* or innate *knowledge*, are the arguments of Book I primarily directed?

A common view is that Locke is primarily against innateness of ideas. One commentator says that 'In the first book Locke argues against the theory of innate ideas, while in the second he gives his own theories about our ideas, their origin and nature'.[1] Another says that Locke's arguments in Book I 'have been designed to prove that none of our ideas are innate . . . . [In Book II he] brings forward the positive side of his theory and proposes to show "whence the understanding may get all the ideas it has" ' [*O'Connor* 41]. But despite such suggestions it is wrong to think that in Book I Locke is attacking innateness of ideas, the materials of knowledge, and that this attack has its complement in Book II's positive account of the origin of ideas in experience. What Locke is primarily rejecting is innateness of knowledge itself. To focus properly on various aspects of the argument in Book I we need to recognise, as a third commentator says, that 'Locke refers us, for the positive complement of [it] . . . not to his theory of the derivation of ideas from experience but to his account of the way in which we may attain to certainty or knowledge' [*Gibson* 33].

What Locke says when he first mentions the 'established opinion' about innateness makes this plain. 'It would', he says,

> be sufficient to convince unprejudiced Readers of the falseness of this Supposition [of innateness], if I should only shew . . . how Men, barely by the Use of their natural Faculties, may attain to all the Knowledge they have, without the help of any innate Impressions; and may arrive at Certainty, without any such Original Notions or Principles. [I.ii.1]

Moreover, Locke's earliest pre-*Essay* references to innateness approach it from the point of view of knowledge itself, not merely ideas. The *Essays on the Law of Nature* portray the doctrine of innateness as about knowledge.[2] When he asks whether there is anything innate, 'written in the souls of men', what is meant is 'whether there are any . . . propositions inborn in the mind' [137]. The same thing is indicated by the very passage used some paragraphs ago to bring out the distinction between ideas, the materials of knowledge, and knowledge itself. We may remember that by using that distinction Locke was able to answer the objection that surely there is some knowledge (for example that every number is either even or odd) which cannot be acquired from experience. But now what lay behind that objection, and hence what Locke was really rejecting, was the thought that such truths, of which we are certain but hardly 'by observation', must be 'innate ideas or Principles'.[3]

Of course there *are* passages which mention innate *ideas*. But their real and underlying concern is with innate *knowledge*. For instance, innate *ideas* figure in the lines immediately following those quoted above from I.ii.1. Yet when the passage is taken as a whole it is plain that they figure merely in an analogy with what Locke has just said about his avowed concern with innate knowledge. There are other places too (I.ii.15, 16, 18, 22, 23, and I.iv) where innate *ideas* are referred to or discussed. But they all turn on the fact that since knowledge presupposes ideas, innate knowledge would presuppose innate ideas. Locke's rejection of innate ideas in these passages is undertaken not for its own sake but as an indirect rejection of innate knowledge.

So the first book of the *Essay* is primarily an attack on innate knowledge or principles, rather than on innate ideas, the materials of knowledge. Against the background of and as a preliminary to describing the original, certainty, and extent of knowledge, Locke wants to reject a certain false account of knowledge. We can now ask exactly what this account is and why he thinks it false.

It is, says Locke, 'an established Opinion amongst some Men, That there are in the Understanding certain *innate Principles*; some primary Notions, κοιναὶ ἔννοιαι, Characters, as it were stamped upon the Mind of Man, which the Soul receives in its very first Being; and brings into the World with it' [I.ii.1]. Following the common practice of the time he divides these principles into the 'speculative' (e.g. ' 'Tis impossible for the same thing to be, and not to be' [I.ii.4]) and the 'practical' (e.g. 'Parents preserve and cherish your Children' [I.iii.12]).⁴ It would be nice if speculative principles were written on our *minds*, and practical ones on our *hearts* or *souls*, for Locke does locate principles in these various places [I.ii.1, iii.8]. Unfortunately there is no such system about it.

The focus of Locke's interest in innateness apparently shifted over the years. Though the early writings of the *Essays on the Law of Nature* and draft B of the *Essay* do refer to speculative principles they are concerned mainly with practical ones. This concern was apparently shared with the adversaries Locke had in mind. He says they assert innateness of 'both practical as well as speculative [principles], and of the former chiefly of the two' [(2) 21]. In the final *Essay*, however, speculative principles had come to be the main target, and Locke no longer characterises his adversaries as being interested chiefly in practical principles [see I.ii.2]. Even so, the *Essay* is concerned with both sorts of principle. Usually Locke's attacks on the two either are simultaneous or have the same structure. We shall first concentrate on the speculative.

Why should anyone think that some of our 'speculative' knowledge is innate? Why should our knowledge that it is impossible for the same thing to be and not to be, be brought into the world with us and not learnt after experience? Locke does not explicitly say why. But if we read between his lines and those of his contemporaries the following answer is suggested. Some of our knowledge, specifically our knowledge of necessary truths, is such that it *could not* have been acquired by observation and experience of the world, *could not* have been learnt. We can explain such knowledge by supposing it innate. How else could we have come to have it? That this is what Locke supposes lies behind and is the rationale for the doctrine of innate principles is suggested by various passages.

The only draft A mention of innate knowledge is in a passage that has already been partly discussed – the one where Locke mentioned against himself an apparent example of knowledge which could not have been derived from experience. Taken as a whole the passage presents the following problem to Locke. Either knowledge is got from experience or it is innate. Some of our knowledge is such that it could not have been acquired from experience. Therefore, some of our knowledge must be innate:

> all our notions and knowledge are not derived . . . from the Ideas taken in by our . . . senses . . . . [There are] certain innate . . . principles of whose truth we are certain though our senses could never come to any observation about them, and soe we could never learne the truth of them from our senses. [(1) 67]

We saw at the beginning of this section that in effect Locke rejects the first premiss of this argument. While he does want to say that ideas or the materials of knowledge are derived from experience he does not want to say that knowledge is. It is, therefore, no real problem for him that one could not have learnt from experience the necessary truth that, for example, all numbers are even or odd. Equally *he* does not, he thinks, have to resort to innateness to explain this knowledge. Nevertheless the passage does suggest that behind the doctrine of innate knowledge was the idea that only it could explain some of our knowledge, our knowledge of necessary truths.[5] This suggestion about the rationale of the doctrine of innatism is supported by passages from two early critics of the *Essay*, James Lowde and Henry Lee.

James Lowde, a Cambridge Fellow and Yorkshire clergyman, was one of the only two critics whom Locke publicly answered. In his *Discourse concerning the nature of Man* (1694), Lowde defends innatism against Locke's strictures [77 f.]. He agrees with the Lockean position that knowledge of necessary truths in 'no ways depends upon Observation' [54]. But *he* then *accepts* innateness, the other half of the above premiss which Locke totally rejects. In explaining the doctrine of 'Natural Inscription' he says:

> our Souls have a native power of finding or framing such Principles or Propositions, the Truth or Knowledge whereof no ways depends upon the evidence of sense or observation: thus knowing what is meant by a whole, and what by a part, hence naturally results the truth of this Proposition [the whole is greater than the parts], without being in any ways oblig'd to sense for it.[53]

Some years later Henry Lee (1622-1713), a clergyman, published an extensive commentary, *Anti-Scepticism: or notes upon each chapter of Mr. Lock's Essay* (1702). Using the same example as Lowde he agrees with Locke that

> There are several *general* Propositions . . . certainly true . . . yet we can come at no Knowledge of them *meerly* by our Senses; because *they* cannot reach to all the Particulars included in the Subjects of them. Our *Senses* may inform us, that any *single* Whole is equal to *all* its Parts; but not that all Wholes in the World are so, unless we could suppose, that we had seen or felt them all.

But then, in a similar vein to Lowde, he continues:

> The *Connexion*, between the Parts of some *general* Propositions, is so *natural* and *indissoluble*, that we can safely judge them to be *true*, without reasoning or casting about for *other* Objects to make their Evidence clearer. I may need a Foot-Measure to satisfie me, that this Room is of the same Length or Breadth with the next; but I need none to satisfie me, that it is of the same Length or Breadth with itself: because nothing can have so near a *Relation* to a thing as *itself*. And therefore such *general* Propositions are call'd *innate*; because . . . certainly and self-evidently true. [43]

This last passage supports our answer to the question, 'Why should anyone think that some knowledge is innate?'. But it shows also that it needs some refinement. It suggests it is insufficiently exact to think simply that innateness was supposed to explain our knowledge of necessary truths in general. It is rather, more specifically, that it was supposed to explain knowledge of *obvious* truths in particular. As Lee indicates, there may be necessary truths which are not obviously true and whose truth appears only when we reason to them from, or see them in the light of, other necessary truths which *do* seem obvious. Many passages in the *Essay* have behind them the idea that Locke's adversaries linked innateness and obvious truth. At one point Locke presents one of his opponents' arguments for innateness. This begins from the fact that many propositions seem obviously true and so receive immediate and universal assent:

> Seeing all Men, even Children, as soon as they hear and understand the Terms, assent to these Propositions, they think it sufficient to prove them innate. For since Men never fail, after they have once understood the Words, to acknowledge them for undoubted truths, they would inferr, That certainly these Propositions were first lodged in the Understanding, which, without any teaching, the Mind at very first Proposal, immediately closes with, and assents to, and after that never doubts again. [I.ii.17]

But though we could now conclude that a connexion was supposed between innateness and obvious truth it may well not be clear in detail just how the link was envisaged. The idea was, I suggest, that the postulated innateness of an obvious truth was meant to explain or be the cause of that proposition's obviousness and ready acceptability. The idea was that if there were, imprinted on our minds, certain principles or propositions then their consequent familiarity and naturalness would explain why we immediately accept them and find them obvious. It should not be surprising if this detail of the connexion between innateness and obviousness is not immediately plain to our twentieth-century eyes. For the current tendency is to suppose that the obviousness of an evident truth must consist in some internal characteristic or feature of self-evidence of the truth itself. Our view is likely to be that we immediately accept some truths simply because we can see, without further thought, that they are indeed true. Whereas a seventeenth-century innatist would explain the evidence, obviousness, and ready acceptability of some propositions by something extrinsic to the propositions themselves, namely their having been imprinted on our minds. According to this view the reason for ready assent to a proposition will not be that it can immediately be seen to be self-evidently true. It will rather be that by virtue of its innateness and imprinting we are 'in sympathy' with it and find it 'natural'.

This explanation of the connexion between innateness and obviousness is merely implicit in Locke's numerous remarks to the effect that 'self-evidence, depend[s] . . . not on innate Impressions, but on something else (as we shall shew hereafter)' [I.ii.18] and that 'this ready Assent of the Mind to some Truths, depends not . . . on Native Inscription' [I.ii.11; also 12, 16, 28, iii.1, II.xi.1]. It is closer to the surface in the criticism of the idea that there are 'first Principles ingrafted in the Minde by Nature' made by another seventeenth-century writer. Richard Burthogge says of 'Propositions which we cannot but assent to as soon as we hear them or minde them' that 'It will appear, if we reflect warily on what doth pass in our Mindes, that even these are not assented to naturally, but (as other Propositions are) judicially'.[6] He thus implies that innatists did suppose ready assent arose from the 'naturalness' or familiarity of a proposition. But that innateness was postulated as an explanatory cause of obviousness and ready assent, is made quite explicit by Lowde. In his defence of innate principles against Locke he considers the objection of another writer, Samuel Parker, to the effect that it was needless of God to imprint obvious and evident truths on our minds: anything that is obvious and self-evident will be recognised and accepted as true without the artificial aid of Divine mental-imprinting. Lowde replies to Parker that unless a truth *were* innately imprinted it *would not be* self-evident. '[T]hese truths do in great measure, owe their clearness and evidence to their being thus imprinted . . . so that the needlessness of imprinting such evident Notions cannot be argued from their present clearness; because it is their being thus imprinted or thus connatural to our minds that makes them so' [57].[7]

Having seen something of why Locke's contemporaries should have thought that some of our 'speculative' knowledge is innate we may now turn to consider Locke's attack on this idea. Its first part, 'No innate speculative Principles' [ii], falls roughly into three parts. Each of these criticises an argument which in

effect begins with a fact or supposed fact about certain propositions, and then proceeds, in the manner we have just been
considering, to postulate their innateness to explain this purported fact. Locke objects to these arguments that the supposed
initial facts to be explained are not really so; that innateness
would anyway not explain them; or that if it would there are
alternative and more plausible explanations to consider.

Thus, says Locke, it is taken for granted that there are certain
principles (both speculative and practical) which are 'universally agreed upon'; and it is taken to follow that these are
'constant Impressions, which . . . Men . . . bring into the
World with them' [I.ii.2], i.e. are innate. But, he argues, innateness is proved only if there is no other way, which surely
there is, of explaining the supposed *universal consent* to these
principles [I.ii.3]. Moreover, the premiss is false and there are
in fact no principles to which 'all Mankind give an Universal
Assent'. Children and idiots, for example, 'have not the least
Apprehension or Thought' of principles as that 'Whatsoever is,
is' [I.ii.4-6].

Locke now portrays the innatists' argument as shifting, in
reaction to this last point, from 'universal assent' to the claim
that everyone assents to these principles 'when they come to the
use of Reason' [I.ii.6]. He consequently replies, first, that defenders of innate knowledge surely do not want to make innate
all the knowledge we come to when we come to the use of reason;
second, that children can reason *before* they know all the principles which *are* supposed to be innate; and, third, that even if
people did assent to them all when they came to the use of
reason this would not prove them innate. '[B]y what kind of
Logick will it appear, that any Notion is Originally by Nature
imprinted in the Mind in its first Constitution, because it comes
first to be observed, and assented to, when a Faculty of the
Mind, which has quite a distinct Province, begins to exert it
self?' [I.ii.14].

Finally Locke considers the argument for innateness which
we have already partly discussed, the argument which begins
from the idea that some propositions are immediately accepted
as soon as they are proposed, i.e. are self-evident.[8] He points out
that, as was the case with the argument from immediate

acceptance by all people who can reason, this argument has unfortunate consequences. If one postulates innateness to explain the obviousness or self-evidence of or immediate assent to some propositions then, in consistency, one has to accept that all such propositions are innate. But there are, he says, many self-evident propositions which no one would *want* to say are innate. No one would want to say that the evident truths that 'White is not Black' and that 'Yellowness is not Sweetness' are innate [I.ii.18].⁹ There are, moreover, many propositions which no one *could* say are innate — because they embody ideas which are derived from experience. '[I]f the Ideas be not innate there was a time, when the Mind was without those Principles. . . . For, where the Ideas themselves are not, there can be no . . . Propositions about them' [I.iv.1]. Locke dwells upon this last point at length. He spends some time, for example, on the question whether the idea of God is innate.

The idea of God is more relevant to practical than it is to speculative principles. But since moral epistemology is not the main concern of the *Essay* I shall deal only briefly with practical principles.

Chapter iii of Book I is devoted specifically to them. Even more than speculative principles practical ones 'come short of an universal Reception' [I.iii.1] as any who are 'but moderately conversant in the History of Mankind' [I.iii.2] would know. Moral practices are, Locke almost zestfully and with some fascination points out, very various. To the suggestion that there are certain moral principles which everyone accepts but simply does not act in accordance with, Locke replies that in these matters surely a man's actions are the best guide to his beliefs. If the acceptance of a practical principle has no effect on practice then how exactly is it a practical principle as opposed to a speculative one? But that practical principles 'come short of an universal Reception' does not mean, says Locke, that they are not true. There *are* true moral principles but they 'require Reasoning and Discourse, and some Exercise of the Mind, to discover the certainty of their Truth' [I.iii.1, 4].

Two things related to this whole discussion of Locke's arguments against innateness should be noted. The first is that in rejecting innateness as an explanatory cause of a proposition's obviousness Locke commits himself to providing an alternative explanation or account of why some propositions are immediately assented to. He is well aware of this commitment and promises to fulfill it [I.ii.3, 11, 12, 16, 18, 28]. We will discuss his explanation later but it should be remembered that the one he rejects explains obviousness in terms of an external property (being imprinted on our minds) which propositions do not have in themselves. His own account is likely to seem more plausible to us for it explains obviousness or self-evidence in terms of an internal characteristic of propositions themselves.

The second point concerns Locke's supposition that there are some self-evident or obvious propositions which even the defenders of innateness would not want to make innate. His opponents would want the truths that 'Whatsoever is, is' [I.ii.4], 'It is impossible for the same thing to be, and not to be' [I.iv.3], and 'the whole is bigger than a part' [I.iv.6] to be innate. But they would not want the truths that red is not blue or that a cat is not a nurse to be so [I.ii.18-21]. Locke does not make clear in a few words why and on what basis only some obvious truths were picked out as innate. But the fact that it was so explains why he refers to the doctrine he is attacking not simply as a doctrine of innate truths but, specifically, as one of innate *principles, maxims* [I.ii.10, 12, 20]. It follows, moreover, that the answer I have suggested to the initial question, 'Why should anyone think that some of our knowledge is innate?', is still too general. We saw first that innateness was connected not simply with knowledge of necessary truths but, more specifically, with a subclass of these, namely obvious truths. We see now that the connexion was with a still smaller class, namely some obvious truths, apparently truths of great generality and abstractness, spoken of as maxims or 'axioms' [IV.vii.1] or 'Principles of Science' [IV.vii.11].

To understand the significance of this we must realise that what faces us here is just one aspect of an extremely important element in Locke's thought. This is his anti-Scholasticism, which recurs throughout the *Essay*. Before going further we must get some general understanding of this anti-Scholasticism which Locke shared with others of his time.

Notes

[1] F. C. Copleston, *A History of Philosophy* (Image Books, New York, 1964), vol.5, part 1, p.82.

[2] Edited by W. von Leyden (Clarendon Press, Oxford, 1954). These essays on the foundations of morality were written in Latin about 1660. They were not published and only a couple of Locke's friends knew of them. They were rediscovered in the 1940s.

[3] Gottfried Wilhelm Leibniz (1646-1716) who, besides much other important, varied and influential work, wrote an extensive commentary on the *Essay*, has this thought in his discussion of Locke [49-50].

[4] Thus, for example, in a reference to innate principles Burthogge [37] distinguishes 'intelligence' and the 'speculative understanding' from 'synteresis' and 'practical understanding'.

[5] Leibniz appears to have this idea in his discussion of Locke and innateness [49-50].

[6] *Burthogge* 38-89. Richard Burthogge (1638?-94?) was a religious and philosophical writer whose *Essay upon Reason, and the Nature of Spirit* (1694) was dedicated to Locke.

[7] Parker (1640-88), Bishop of Oxford, wrote on philosophical, political, historical and ecclesiastical matters. His discussion of innate ideas is in *A Free and Impartial Censure of the Platonick Philosophie* (1666) which we will meet again in section 6.

[8] I.ii.18 and 21 make plain the connexion between immediate acceptance and self-evidence.

[9] Lowde [54] refers to these very examples (without mention of Locke) and says 'we may easily discern a difference betwixt the Truth of such Propositions, as these [the whole is bigger than the parts], and those others, which are brought by some to vie with those natural Notions, *viz. White is not black, Yellowness is not sweetness, etc.*' [53-4]. Then later, referring to Locke directly, he tries to answer him. The difference he sees is that the truth of these others 'depends upon the actual existence of Things' [81].

4 'Ancients' versus 'Moderns'

Two conflicting currents ran through the intellectual life of the seventeenth century. As the title of an important book has it, the thought of the time can very usefully be seen as a battle between the 'ancients' and the 'moderns' [*Jones*]. The 'ancients' were referred to by various names: Scholastics, Schoolmen, Peripatetics, Aristotelians. They belonged to a tradition which had its source in the works of the classical Greek philosopher Aristotle (384-322 B.C.). The modernism, which set itself energetically and insistently against this prevailing and ancient tradition, found one of its earliest and most influential expressions in England in the writings of Francis Bacon (1561-1626), Lord Chancellor and man of public affairs. His philosophical and methodological writings, such as *Advancement of Learning* (1605) and *Novum Organum* (1620), contain a grand vision of a revived and renewed science based on extensive collaboration. As the modern movement, taking much of its inspiration from Bacon, gathered momentum it carried along with it most of the best known names of the time.

According to its 'modern' critics the whole scheme of traditional learning had nothing to offer. It was devoid of substance and significance, and at a sterile standstill. In passages which capture this new attitude and set its tone, Bacon claimed that the 'variety of books with which the arts and sciences abound' are filled solely with 'endless repetitions of the same thing, varying in the method of treatment, but not new in substance, insomuch that the whole stock, numerous as it appears at first view, proves on examination to be but scanty'. Nothing was being added to what had gone before, no new developments had occurred, empty controversy had taken the place of constructive argument:

> that wisdom which we have derived principally from the Greeks is but like the boyhood of knowledge, and has the characteristic property of boys: it

can talk, but it cannot generate; for it is fruitful of controversies but barren of works. . . . [I]f sciences of this kind had any life in them, that could never come to pass which has been the case now for many ages – that they stand almost at a stay, without receiving any augmentations worthy of the human race; insomuch that many times not only what was asserted once is asserted still, and instead of being resolved by discussion is only fixed and fed. [4.13-14]

Some years later John Webster, thinking in particular of its theology, asked about the still prevailing Scholasticism, 'what is it else but a confused *Chaos*, of needless, frivolous, fruitless, triviall, vain, curious, impertinent, knotty, ungodly, irreligious thorny, and hel-hate'th disputes, altercations, doubts, questions and endless janglings?' [15].[1]

From time to time, as the occasion arises, we shall need to consider in detail particular doctrines of the ancient tradition to which the moderns took exception. But their objections did not focus solely on the content of the traditional teaching. They focussed also on the attitude people had taken towards it. There was, it was felt, an undue and unthinking respect for accepted authority. The typical mental attitude was taken to be one of subserviency and conservatism. Minds were enslaved by the past, for what it taught was taken on trust. Received doctrine was handed down and unquestioningly adopted, improperly assimilated, left undigested by the juices of living and individual understanding. Men, complains Bacon, 'have been kept back as by a kind of enchantment from progress in the sciences by reverence for antiquity, by the authority of men accounted great in philosophy, and then by general consent' [4.81-2]. As a result, 'Philosophy and the intellectual sciences . . . stand like statues, worshipped and celebrated, but not moved or advanced' [4.14].

Part of Locke's animus against the doctrine of innate knowledge derives from the idea that it encourages, particularly in its connexion with moral or practical principles, an unthinking reliance on authority and second-hand opinion at the expense of genuine individual understanding. Bacon had observed that people prefer things to be reduced to a neat system or formula because 'it makes the work short and easy, and saves further inquiry' [4.15]. Locke similarly complains that the theory of

Locke

innateness 'being once received . . . eased the lazy from the pains of search' [I.iv.24].

Locke thought that these undesirable effects of the doctrine of innateness come about in the following way. There are things which each grown person is naturally inclined to believe. Certain of his opinions and beliefs are instilled in him from an early age and are continually confirmed by those around him. Because he has no memory of how these beliefs originated it is easy for him to take them to be innate. But once he has taken them this way he will then be 'afraid to question those Principles'. For 'he shall think them, as most Men do, the Standards set up by God in his Mind, to be the Rule and Touchstone of all other Opinions' [I.iii.25; also 22-4, IV.xx.8-10]. The whole process is reinforced by a disinclination or lack of time to question, reconsider, and make up one's own mind for oneself, and by the fact that people need things to believe in [I.iii.24-6]. Even if more people could live 'without employing their time in the daily Labours of their Callings' [I.iii.24] and had the leisure to reflect and question, there is hardly anyone 'that dare shake the foundations of all his past Thoughts and Actions, and endure to bring upon himself, the shame of having been a long time wholly in mistake and error . . . . Who is there, hardy enough to contend with the reproach which is every where prepared for those, who dare venture to dissent from the received Opinions of their Country or Party?' [I.iii.25].

Locke believes the doctrine of innateness stops people thinking for themselves. It thus tends to support the current orthodoxy of established parties and factions [I.iii.20]. Once it is accepted that there are innate principles people are 'put . . . upon a necessity of receiving some Doctrines as such; which was to take them off from the use of their own Reason and Judgement, and put them upon believing and taking them upon trust without farther examination' [I.iv.24]. It was of prime importance for Locke that people should seek after truth and see it, wherever it lay, for themselves. Their beliefs should be determined by what they see to be true, not by what is handed down to them. The passages in which this thought finds expression are amongst the most passionately eloquent of any Locke wrote:

Not that I want a due respect to other Mens Opinions; but after all, the greatest reverence is due to Truth . . . [W]e may as rationally hope to see with other Mens Eyes, as to know by other Mens Understandings . . . . The floating of other Mens Opinions in our brains makes us not one jot the more knowing, though they happen to be true. . . . Aristotle was certainly a knowing Man, but no body ever thought him so, because he blindly embraced, and confidently vented the Opinions of another. [I.iv.23; also (4) 94, (5) 3.269]

In his attacks on innateness Locke is therefore not only removing what he takes to be a false account of knowledge. He is also, and in sympathy with one of the prevailing moods of the century, expressing deep concern for individual judgement as against the deadness of received opinion and second-hand dogma.

Well over half a century earlier Bacon was quite convinced that a radical solution was needed for the unsatisfactory state of intellectual affairs which stemmed from the prevelance of and reverence for ancient tradition. It was not enough to tamper and tinker with established ways of thinking and with received doctrine. Things could not be changed 'by a preposterous subtlety and winnowing of argument . . . . [T]his comes too late, the case being already past remedy; and is far from setting the business right or sifting away the errors' [4.28]. The intellectual edifices of the past needed to be thoroughly and cleanly swept away. A fresh beginning had to be made with new methods and new foundations. 'The only hope', said Bacon, 'lies in a recon-struction of the sciences' [4.28]. Nothing less would do than 'to try the whole thing anew upon a better plan, and to commence a total reconstruction of the sciences, arts, and all human know-ledge, raised upon the proper foundations' [4.8].

Bacon's energetic impatience with the sterilities of Scholas-ticism and his belief in radical reconstruction captured the imagination of the century. It was taken up in a fresh and lively fashion by a chorus of enthusiastic voices. Their favourite metaphors were of rubbish-clearing, laying new foundations, reconstruction and rebuilding. Thus in 1663 Henry Power (1623-68), physician and natural philosopher, described the age as one where

Philosophy comes in with a Spring-tide; and the Peripateticks may as well hope to stop the Current of the Tide, or . . . to fetter the Ocean, as hinder the overflowing of free Philosophy: Me-thinks, I see how all the old Rubbish must be thrown away, and the rotten Buildings be overthrown and carried away with so powerful an Inundation. These are the days that must lay a new Foundation of a more magnificent Philosophy, never to be overthrown. [192]

In 1668 Joseph Glanvill too thought in terms of the removing of rubbish and the preparation for rebuilding.[2] John Webster also, in 1663, refers to the 'rotten and ruinous fabric of Aristotle' and to the 'building up of a well-grounded and lasting Fabrick' [105]. Similarly Thomas Sprat (1635-1713), Dean of Westminster and man of letters, unhappy in 1667 that 'the *Antients* should still possess a Tyranny over our Judgements' speaks of the ground being made 'open, and cleer' and of 'remov'd . . . rubbish', which 'when one great Fabrick is to be pull'd down, and another erected in its stead, is always esteemed well nigh half the whole work' [28-9]. This background gives a depth of richness and meaning to the splendidly written and rightly famous under-labourer passage in Locke's 'Epistle to the Reader'. The passage is a classical expression of the 'modernist' sentiment and is worth quoting at length:

The commonwealth of Learning, is not at this time without Master-Builders, whose mighty Designs, in advancing the Sciences, will leave lasting Monuments to the Admiration of Posterity; But every one must not hope to be a Boyle, or a Sydenham; and in an Age that produces such Masters, as the Great Huygenius, and the incomparable Mr. Newton, with some other of that Strain; 'tis Ambition enough to be employed as an Under-Labourer in clearing Ground a little, and removing some of the Rubbish, that lies in the way to Knowledge; which certainly had been very much more advanced in the World, if the Endeavours of ingenious and industrious Men had not been much cumbred with the learned but frivolous use of uncouth, affected, or unintelligible Terms, introduced into the Sciences, and there made an Art of, to that Degree, that Philosophy, which is nothing but the true Knowledge of Things, was thought unfit, or uncapable to be brought into well-bred Company, and polite Conversation. Vague and insignificant Forms of Speech, and Abuse of Language, have so long passed for Mysteries of Science . . . . To break in upon the Sanctuary of Vanity and Ignorance, will be, I suppose, some Service to Humane Understanding. [9-10]

One objection in particular was frequently made to Scholasticism. It had failed to produce much in the way of a body of knowledge about nature and its phenomena. 'The *Aristotelian Philosophy*', says Glanvill, 'is inept for New discoveries' [(1) 178]. It does not, says Webster, have 'sufficient keyes to open the Cabinet of Natures rich treasurie' [92]. So what Bacon and his intellectual heirs had in mind when they spoke of 'the proper foundation' of the 'sciences, arts, and all human knowledge' was a mass of information about the natural world which would be derived from and based upon 'labour and pains, experiments and operations, tryals, and observations' [*Webster* 92].

This belief in careful painstaking observation and methodical experiment as the 'proper foundation' of knowledge had a complement in a barrage of complaints about the emptiness and sterility of Scholastic teaching. The two together produced a critical contrast which was extremely common in seventeenth-century writings. This was the contrast between *words* and *things*, between useless mental speculation, and concrete realities and facts. Bacon made a point of saying that he sought for truth not in the mind, but in the world [4.19, 21, 24]. Glanvill described the Aristotelian Philosophy as 'an huddle of *words* and *terms insignificant*', as 'a *Philosophy*, that makes most accurate Inspections into the *Creatures* of the *Brain*', whose 'Basis and Superstructure are *Chimaerical*'. Its '*Verbosities* do emasculate the *Understanding*' and 'the Things themselves [get] lost in a crowd of *Names*' [(1) 150-1]. Scholasticism 'is meerly verbal, speculative, abstractive, formal and notional', unrelated to reality; one must abandon all that clutter and turn to things, facts, observations, to 'experimental manduction into the more interiour clossets of nature' [*Webster* 67; also 33, 85, 92, 102]. One must turn from the study to the world. One must turn, said Robert Hooke, from 'work of the Brain and the Fancy' to 'the plainness and soundness of observations on material and obvious things' [5].[3] The Scholastics, says Webster, use 'no better helps for searching into natures abstruse secrets than the *Chymaeras* of their own brains', they 'onely make a mold and *Idaea* in their heads, and never go out by industrious searches, and observant experimen:s, to find out the mysteries contained in nature' [92]. Similarly Sprat says that one should not concentrate on 'thoughts and words', 'things that are . . . out of the world', but should begin with 'Works', with observations and experiment [336]. If we do 'The Beautiful Bosom of *Nature* will be Expos'd to our view: we shall enter into its *Garden*, and taste of its *Fruits*, and satisfy our selves with its *plenty*; insteed of Idle talking, and wandring, under its fruitless shadows; as the *Peripatetics* did in their first institution, and their Successors have done ever since'.[4]

In view of these recommendations of the anti-Scholastics for things as against words it should not be surprising that one of the fruits of the 'modernist' movement has been a fairly systematic and organised body of knowledge and theory about the workings and phenomena of the natural world. Natural science as we have it today is to an important extent a production of the very intellectual movements we are considering. We should consider this fact in more detail.

One of the pillars of the orthodox scientific establishment in England now is the Royal Society. To be elected as a fellow, or F.R.S., is a mark of the highest prestige. But the Royal Society of London for the Improving of Natural Knowledge has (along with parallel societies in other European countries) its origin in the intellectual revolutions of the seventeenth century. It was one of the more conspicious and immediately tangible products of the anti-traditionalism of the period, and its early reception was hardly so smooth as its present standing might lead one to expect. Both in its earliest days and after 1662 when King Charles II had given it the seal of approval of a Royal Charter, it formed the focus of the new attitudes and ways of thought, the stress on observation and experiment in particular, and was a stronghold of anti-Scholasticism.[5] Not long after 1662 Thomas Sprat was commissioned to write *The History* of the Royal Society, of which he became a fellow in 1663. It was prefaced by an ode by the poet Abraham Cowley (1618-67), himself an enthusiast for the new movement. The ode speaks of philosophy and human knowledge having been 'kept in Nonage till of late', by people who, jealous of their authority, concentrated on words rather than on things, on 'sports of wanton Wit', on 'Pageants of the Brain', rather than on 'The Riches which do hoorded . . . lye/In Natures endless Treasurie'.

The connexion of the modernist anti-Scholastic movement with the development of modern experimental science can be found in Locke's 'rubbish clearing' passage which was quoted earlier. Its connexion with the Royal Society can also be found there. The 'master-builders', Newton, Boyle, Sydenham, Huygens, with whom Locke compares himself so modestly as an 'under-labourer' all have their place, as Locke predicted, in the history of science. All went in for careful experiments, meticulous and methodical observations, or for the construction of theories which systematised or explained such experiments and observations. All but one, moreover, were associated with the Royal Society.

'The incomparable Mr. Newton' (1642-1727) was elected as a fellow of the Royal Society in 1672, and as President in 1703. The most notable of his scientific achievements is his theory of universal gravitation published in his *Philosophiae Naturalis Principia Mathematica* (1687). Locke and Newton knew each other well, after meeting in 1689. Robert Boyle (1627-91) was connected with the Royal Society from its very earliest days, and was elected its President in 1680. He is known as 'the father of modern chemistry' and is perhaps best remembered for his work on the expansion of gases. He devised an air-pump and developed the barometer as a weather indicator. Thomas Sydenham (1624-89) is an exception in this group only in that he was never a fellow of the Royal Society. He has a significant place in the history of medicine, particularly because of his observations on the spread of epidemic diseases and his work on the treatment of smallpox. Finally, Christiaan Huygens (1629-95), a distinguished Dutch mathematician, astronomer, and physicist became an F.R.S. in 1663. He did important work on the collision of elastic bodies and lectured on this subject to the Royal Society in 1669.

Locke himself belongs to this group of 'virtuosi', as the seventeenth century called those who took part in the activities of the Royal Society and busied themselves with its new ideas. He had a direct first-order interest in the workings of the natural world of just the sort these master-builders had. He became interested in medicine as early as 1652 when still an Oxford undergraduate. Though he formally qualified only in 1674, he in fact practised it from 1666 to the end of his life. Much of his correspondence was to and from doctors who often consulted him on their own cases. He met Thomas Sydenham in 1667, the year after the Great Plague and shortly after he had arrived in London as Lord Ashley's physician. It has been suggested that Sydenham was one of those present at the meeting of friends where the seeds of the *Essay* were sown. Locke collaborated with him both in his practical and in his written work, *Observationes Medicae* (1676), on infectious diseases.

Locke's interests were not limited to physiology and the practical treatment of illness. He had a lifelong friendship with Robert Boyle whom he first met in 1660 in Oxford where Boyle had been for some years a member of the experimental science club which was a precursor of the London Royal Society. This friendship must have stimulated an interest in chemistry and the preparation of medicines. He also had a concern with weather observation. Many of his observations were incorporated into Boyle's *General History of the Air* (1692) which Locke prepared for publication. He did not make the observations simply for their own sake. He was mindful of the possibility of a connexion between climatic conditions and the occurrence of epidemics.

Despite these abiding and serious interests in physical and medical matters Locke was not a 'naturalist' of the order of his friends and collaborators Boyle and Sydenham. Unlike them he has no important place in the history of science. He was, nevertheless, elected fellow of the Royal Society in 1668, and was put on a committee for 'considering and directing experiments'. There was, however, no expectation then as there is now that an F.R.S. would have made a distinctive and weighty contribution to the experimental or theoretical sciences. It has been estimated that in its early days only about one third of Royal Society fellows were 'scientific men'. The rest were 'those who might be interested in the new philosophy and its aims' [*Lyons* 52].

If this seems surprising we should remember that when it was first formed the Royal Society provided a focus for a whole general movement of thought. Though modern science doubtless is one of the more conspicuous products of that movement the Society was not narrowly restricted to science in any modern sense. It was more broadly philosophical, and encapsulated a generalised dissatisfaction with Scholasticism and traditional learning. Its motto 'Nullius in Verba' – 'in the words of no one else' – summarised this overall rejection of the authority of the past. It must be realised, moreover, that the apparently simple fact that the natural science of later centuries is a product of that time has a hidden complexity to it. It is not as though there always was a clear conception of what such a science would be like and as though all that was lacking was a success in producing it. It is rather than the very idea of a body of knowledge about the world of the sort we have now, the very idea of a natural science, was being forged at the time. As we shall see in more detail in later sections, knowledge, as the seventeenth century understood it, was not something which could be obtained from such an observation-based study of the workings of the natural world. The study itself was not called natural science but natural philosophy. Science, as the seventeenth century understood it, was not something that could result from activities of the sort advocated by the Royal Society. This meant that the new 'natural philosophy' stood in need of more than merely practical development. It stood also in need of intellectual defences. Not merely science but also the *idea* of science was at issue. 'Today science is so securely entrenched that the intellectual concept upon which it is based is almost ignored, and discoveries alone are valued, but in the seventeenth century the concept, new and in need of protection, was the greater concern' [*Jones* 184].

It need not be surprising, then, that Locke, who has gone down in history as a philosopher rather than as a scientist, should have been a fellow of the Royal Society of London for the Improving of Natural Knowledge. Even had he had no talent as a scientific experimentalist or theoretician there would have been no problem about his election. For one thing he belonged as a member of the modern movement in general. More importantly, however, he belonged also as one who developed and provided intellectual defences for the newly emerging conception of natural science. As we shall see in some detail, the *Essay* contains much in the way of explanation and justification of the methods of the new experimentalism. Locke's claim to be an under-labourer to Boyle and Newton should not be seen merely as a rhetorical flourish.

The works of the virtuosi, the 'modernists' of the seventeenth century, sometimes make it difficult to see that anything could be said in favour of the Scholasticism they attacked. Particularly in their critical polemical passages, they have a freshness and directness, such confidence that the world is now *their* oyster, that it seems besides the point to wonder what might have been said in defence of their opponents. But there *was* something to be said. For example, in his *Letter . . . concerning Natural experimental philosophie* (1669)[6] Meric Casaubon (1599-1671), a classical scholar who wrote extensively, made out a good case for supposing there to be much of human value in the tradition he wished to defend. Along with others at the time he criticised the stress the virtuosi laid on observation and experiment on the grounds that it is likely to lead to atheism. 'Men that are much fixed upon matter . . . may . . . forget that there be such things in the world as *Spirits* . . . and, at last, that there is a God, and that their souls are immortal'.[7] He advocated '*Notional*' studies which have 'nothing to do with the senses' and are 'therefore the more divine' [30]. He also suggested that an undue concentration on investigation of the natural world may lead to a certain intellectual arrogance. '[M]ay not a man go too far in this study, and overvalue his progress so far, as to think nothing out of his reach?' [34]. In one way this objection is misplaced for we have already seen in section 2 that Locke and others in the modern movement were able to retain an element of scepticism about man's ability to know. We shall see in section 15 that there is no arrogance in Locke's evaluation of man's intellectual capabilities. In another way, however, Casaubon is right. He is right to suggest that the experimental philosopher is in danger of supposing that all areas of human concern and experience are legitimate grist for his mill. Casaubon reports a story which illustrates the absurdity of this arrogance of the specialist and teaches a lesson which is just as applicable today as it was then.

A man who watched a fight between a louse and a flea through a microscope claimed to have learnt from it self-

control, temperance, and forbearance, and to have 'profited
more to rule his passions in the rest of his life, than he had done
by any thing he had heard, or read before'.

Casaubon ridicules
the idea that collecting straightforward data about fleas and lice
can provide the moral and civilising education of the sort given
by a study of works of humane literature written by wise and
sensitive men. He sarcastically remarks that no doubt the story
was in fact made up 'to gratifie some friends, who would be glad
to hear what use can be made, even in point of life and manners,
of a *microscope*' [31-3].

To an extent the Scholastics can even be defended against the
common critical jibe that they neglected observation and experiment as legitimate sources of knowledge. According to a
recent historian 'only those unfamiliar with [some of their] . . .
actual works . . . would accuse the scholastics of having given *no*
thought to sense-experience' [*Wiener* 596]. Some of the criticisms made in this direction may have been rather wild. But we
should not forget the background against which they were
made. It was not as though the Scholastics had our idea of a
natural science and, for some curious reason, neglected to seek
such science in the appropriate way, i.e. on the basis of observation and experiment. It was rather that, as we saw above, our
idea of an experimentally and observationally based science of
nature was only then being forged. Embodied in the jibes of the
'moderns' is their new idea of 'natural philosophy', a systematic
and far-reaching study of nature. Embodied there too are the
seeds of a new conception of what can properly be called
'science', of what is an acceptable result for man's intellectual
endeavours. The conflict is a basic one with a traditional and
ancient conception of what ideally 'science' is. This older view
about the shape of a systematic body of knowledge of the sort
man ought to aim for derives from Aristotle's theory of *scientia* or
demonstrative knowledge. We shall look at it in passing in the
next section and in detail in section 7.

Notes

1   Webster (1610-82), chemist and religious writer, argued in his *Academiarum Examen* (1654) for a reformed education system which would develop new learning freed from the past.

2   *Plus Ultra* (1668: reprinted Scholars' Facsimiles, Gainsville, Florida, 1958), p.91; also (1) 72-3.

3   Hooke (1635-1703), author of *Micrographia* (1665), contributed to many areas of science such as physics and astronomy. He assisted Boyle in the construction of his air-pump. He was elected fellow of the Royal Society in 1663.

4   *Sprat* 327; also 326, 336, 341, verse 4 of the prefatory ode; *Glanvill* (1) 148 f.

5   For its history see *Lyons* and Margery Purver, *The Royal Society: Concept and Creation* (Routledge and Kegan Paul, London, 1967).

6   Reprinted in M.R.G. Spiller, *Concerning Natural Experimental Philosophie* (Martinus Nijhoff, The Hague, 1980).

7   See end of section 17 and R.S. Westfall, *Science and Religion in Seventeenth-Century England* (Yale University Press, New Haven, 1958), pp. 21 f.

5 Innatism in Context

The last section gave a general account of conflicting currents in seventeenth-century intellectual activity. This account was needed as a background to a proper understanding of Locke's rejection of innate principles and knowledge. Concerning this rejection our conclusion at the end of section 3 was that though the idea that they might be innate was used to explain why certain necessary truths seemed obviously true this explanation was not given for *all* self-evident truths. It was given, specifically, in connexion with a small class of self-evident truths which were spoken of as 'maxims', 'axioms', 'principles'. An example Locke gives is 'That it is impossible for the same thing to be and not to be'. Apparently, then, 'maxims' or 'principles' are self-evident truths *of great generality and abstractness*. In fact they form an element of the Aristotelian theory of *scientia* or scientific demonstration which was mentioned at the end of the last section. This theory will be explained more fully in section 8, but in order to complete our discussion of Locke's attacks on innateness something must be said about it now.

'Scientia', the word used in Latin texts of Aristotle of the sort used in the seventeenth century, might be translated as 'knowledge'. But, as remarked in the last section, what seventeenth-century philosophers understood by 'knowledge' was not quite what we do now. To understand their idea we need to understand the Aristotelian theory of *scientia*. For a long time that theory in effect *defined* what 'knowledge' is. Scientific knowledge according to this theory is of 'that which is necessary [and] cannot be otherwise'.[1] It is to be contrasted with 'opinion' which is of contingencies which may or may not be, or which may be otherwise.

A further feature of 'knowledge', one which particularly concerns us here, is that it is conceived as having a certain structure. Items of *scientia* or scientific knowledge are not isolated, but are related in the following way. Much of what we know presupposes something else we know from which it is derived. Knowledge advances by our deriving new propositions from and in accordance with certain 'axioms' or 'principles' which lie at the basis of our derived or demonstrated knowledge. These axioms themselves can hardly be derived by reason and are, in Aristotle's view, acquired from sense-experience, by means of a faculty of 'intellectual intuition'.

What is of particular interest in the present connexion is that it was sometimes held in the seventeenth century that these basic 'principles' are innate. Chillingworth speaks of there being 'common notions written by God in the hearts of all men'. He speaks too of our 'deducing according to the never-failing rules of logic, consequent deductions from them'.[2] Glanvill uses as examples exactly what a reading of Locke would lead us to expect and refers to certain 'foundation-*Propositions*', 'certain *congenite propositions*; which I conceive to be the very *Essentials* of Rationality' [(1) 97-8]. Similarly, Burthogge, though critical of it, discusses the idea that there is 'a System of Notions and first Principles ingrafted in the Minde by Nature, in whose Light all others were to shine and to be seen'.[3]

So the terms 'axioms' and 'principles' which appear in Locke's discussion of the doctrine of innateness belong with an Aristotelian account of *scientia* or scientific knowledge. Furthermore, as we will see in section 8, Locke explicitly attacks that account. We might expect then that his interest in criticising innateness connects with his dissatisfaction with the Scholastic account of knowledge. This is indeed so. There are passages in the Book I discussions of innateness which make clear reference to the Scholastic theory of demonstrative knowledge or which refer us forwards to the later chapter [IV.vii] where that theory is explicitly attacked [I.ii.9, 20, 27; iv.21]. Conversely, there are passages in this later chapter, 'On maxims', which refer back to Book I [See particularly (2) 113]. We should notice, too, that Locke's very descriptions of the doctrine of innateness he is attacking in Book I sometimes connect it with the Aristotelian theory of *scientia*. For example, he describes innate principles as being 'woven into the very Principles of their [men's] Being,

and imprinted there in indelible Characters, to be the Foundation, and Guide of all their acquired Knowledge, and future
Reasonings' [I.ii.25]. He says they are supposed to be 'imprinted by Nature, as the Foundation and Guide of our Reason'
[I.ii.10].

Even after Locke's attacks on them, innate principles were
not short of defenders [*Yolton* 48 ff.]. It was repeatedly said that
Locke portrays innateness in too crude a fashion. Why suppose
that one is born with certain principles already imprinted on
the mind? It is merely that one is born with a mind shaped,
disposed, or inclined to formulate these principles later, perhaps on the occasion of sensory stimuli. Lowde, one of the first
to respond to Locke, objected to this misinterpretation of the
theory and makes the point that 'the Defendent has always
leave to state his own Question, and to declare in what sense he
undertakes the defence of it'.[4] He then explains in defence of
innateness that 'These natural Notions are not so imprinted
upon the Soul, as that they naturally and necessarily exert
themselves . . . without any assistance from the outward
Senses, or without the help of some previous Cultivation' [52-3].

A question frequently asked is: Who exactly was Locke attacking when he attacked the doctrine of innate knowledge?
The one person he mentions by name, Lord Herbert, is mentioned only as someone whose work (*De Veritate*) he consulted
'When I had writ this' [I.iii.15]. Therefore he can hardly have
been the prime target. It is commonly suggested that Locke had
Descartes in mind. But though Descartes did have a doctrine of
innateness it mainly concerned *ideas*; whereas Locke was, we
have seen, primarily attacking an innateness of *knowledge*. What
we have learnt here supports Gibson's suggestion that Locke
'conceived himself to be engaged in conflict with the current
procedure of the Schools' [41], i.e. the Aristotelian or Scholastic
account of knowledge. He attacks a doctrine of innateness
because he finds that it stands in the way of what he himself
wants to say, not about ideas the materials of knowledge, but
about knowledge itself. This doctrine is connected, as Locke
himself brings to our attention, with the Scholastic idea of
scientia. It is very likely of course that had he been asked Locke

might have named people who held the sort of view he opposed. But we need not suppose that there was anyone he had specifically in mind as he wrote.

Notes

1   *Posterior Analytics* 88b32. Quotations from Aristotle are from W.D. Ross' ·edition of *The Works of Aristotle* (Clarendon Press, Oxford, 1908-52) but the references are standard.
2   *Religion of the Protestants* (1638), p.8. William Chillingworth (1602-44) was a theologian who argued for the primacy of individual reason and the Scriptures as against the authority of the Church.
3   *Burthogge* 38; see also *Boyle* 4.445 and Edward Reynolds, *Treatise of the Passions and Faculties of the Soule of Man* (1640), pp. 455-6.
4   *Lowde* 52. The words 'defendent' and 'question' are terms from the Scholastic idea of a disputation (see section 8).

6 Ideas: The Materials of Knowledge

We have seen how in Book I Locke criticises and rejects one view about the origin of knowledge. According to it at least some of our knowledge is innate. In Book II he develops his own alternative. The essence of this is that 'all our Knowledge is founded; and . . . ultimately derives it self' *from experience* [II.i.2]. We saw that when Locke stated this view in draft A, he reported the objection that surely there was some knowledge, our knowledge of necessary truths, which could not be derived from experience. He replied by distinguishing between ideas, the materials of knowledge, and knowledge itself. He then made it plain that what initially is derived from experience is merely ideas, not knowledge itself.

It is unfortunate that this objection and reply were not written into the final *Essay* for it was repeated by more than one reader. Lee said that 'If all Knowledge comes . . . [from experience] which is his [Locke's] Maxim, then there can be no *certain* Knowledge of the Truth of any *general* Proposition whatever; because our Senses can reach but to particulars' [67].

But not everyone would have seen anything to criticise Locke for here. There were some who believed that knowledge of such truths *could* be gained from experience in just the way Lee (and Locke) thought it could not. Parker's view was that

> *general Axioms* are only the results and abridgments of a multitude of single Experiments; thus from the plain experience and observation of all mankind was framed that unquestionable maxime, *That the whole is greater than its parts*, because they saw and found it was so in all individual Bodies in the world, and the Reason why all men assent to it at the first proposal, is because they cannot look abroad, but they are presented with innumerable instances thereof, every visible thing in the world being a *whole* compounded of parts sensibly smaller than itself.[1]

In general, however, there was agreement with Lee (and Locke) that knowledge of this sort could *not* come from experience. The conclusion was then drawn, for example by Lowde [54] and by Leibniz [50], that knowledge of such truths must be innate.

Locke, of course, does not draw *this* conclusion. There is a subtlety in his position. He does not accept that a piece of knowledge must either be innate or else must come from experience. Though he denies that any of our knowledge is innate, he also denies that it comes directly or immediately from experience. What do come directly from experience are ideas. But these do not themselves constitute knowledge. They are merely the materials out of which all knowledge is constructed. The explanation of how knowledge is indirectly derived from experience will concern us in the next section. For the moment we should focus our attention on ideas, on what they are and how they are acquired.

Locke's contemporaries criticised him for his constant talk of 'ideas'. Edward Stillingfleet (1635-99), the Bishop of Worcester, who engaged him in long public controversy about the *Essay*, often refers disparagingly to the 'new way of ideas'.[2] And Lee wondered whether 'instead of advancing *Humane Knowledge*, this new *Ideal Language* will not rather *confound* that little Knowledge we have' [1].[3] The term 'idea' has played a part in philosophy at least as far back as Plato, but Locke's use of it is derived from Descartes. There is a lot to be said about the 'new ideal language' of the seventeenth century, much more than there is room to say here.[4]

Locke in fact apologises for his 'frequent use of the Word *Idea*'. He then explains it stands for 'whatsoever is the Object of the Understanding when a Man thinks' and expresses 'whatever is meant by *Phantasm, Notion, Species*'[I.i.8]. The terminology of phantasms, notions, and species, is basically Scholastic and figured in earlier discussions of memory, imagination, sensation, perception and thought. Though in many respects it needs explaining this passage from a famous seventeenth-century Scholastic, Franco Burgersdijck (1590-1636), professor of logic at Leiden, illustrates some of these uses. 'Intelligible species of singular things are impressed in the intellect by phantasms quite similar to the way in which phantasms are impressed in the internal sense by those species which are formed in the external sense by the objects'.[5]

It thus comes about that we find Locke using the word 'idea' in various contexts. He speaks of 'the Ideas got by Sensation' which are 'the Impressions that are made on our Senses by outward Objects' [II.i.24; also 23]. When we see a moving object the mind 'takes in' the ideas of motion and colour [II.ii.1] and when fire burns our bodies the 'sence of Heat, or Idea of Pain' may be 'produced in the Mind' [II.ix.2]. He says furthermore that 'Memory . . . is as it were the Store-house of our Ideas' [II.x.2]. And then, in connexion with the intellect rather than with the senses, he says that 'Every Man being conscious to himself, That he thinks, and that which his Mind is employ'd about whilst thinking, being the Ideas, that are there, 'tis past doubt, that Men have in their Minds several Ideas' [II.i.1]. Also in connexion with the intellect he says that words 'in every Man's Mouth, stand for the Ideas he has, and which he would express by them' [III.ii.3]. Ideas, then, can be internal sensations like pain, and they can be perceptions of external objects and their qualities. They can be the medium of memory, and they can figure in thinking and the understanding of language. Given all of this there is little wonder that John Sergeant found Locke's term 'idea' to be equivocal and criticised him for 'the promiscuous usage of that Word in such Disparate Senses'.[6]

Shortly after the publication of the *Essay* Norris raised the question of 'what kind of things [Locke] makes these Ideas to be as to their *Essence* or *Nature*'.[7] What he was trying to discover was whether Locke's ideas were states or modifications of the mind (like waves on the sea) or whether they were mental entities in their own right (like flotsam on the sea). Plato had spoken of ideas as being completely independent of minds. For him they had a reality of their own quite apart from any relation they might have to mind. But since Descartes began to speak of them in connexion with minds the question about the exact nature of their relationship to minds had been in the air. But Locke himself seems to have been uninterested in it. In the comments he made on Norris' book he is impatient with him for raising it. He says that, whatever the answer to it is, it is of little consequence to anything he wants to say [(5) 10.248, 256].

In one way or another, then, ideas are what occupy our

minds. In Locke's view they are all, without exception, acquired from experience. Prior to experience the mind is 'white Paper, void of all Characters, without any Ideas' [II.i.2]. 'Experience', however, is not one single source of ideas, but two. In the first place there is sensation. 'Our Senses, conversant about particular sensible Objects, do convey into the Mind, several distinct Perceptions of things . . . [a]nd thus we come by those Ideas, we have of Yellow, White, Heat, Cold, Soft, Hard, Bitter, Sweet' [II.i.3]. Then there is *reflection*, which is the 'Perception of the Operations of our own Minds within us, as it is employ'd about the Ideas it has got; which Operations, when the Soul comes to reflect on, and consider, do furnish the Understanding with another set of Ideas . . . Perception, Thinking, Doubting, Believing, Reasoning, Knowing, Willing' [II.i.4]. Locke states quite categorically that there is no source of ideas but these two. Our understanding has not 'the least glimmering of any Ideas, which it doth not receive from one of these two. External objects furnish the Mind with the Ideas of sensible qualities, which are all those different perceptions they produce in us: And the Mind furnishes the Understanding with Ideas of its own operations' [II.i.5]. In all strictness, however, it should perhaps be said that sensation and reflection are the only *natural* sources of ideas. For on occasions Locke seems, as he thought about the matter more, to have wanted to allow the possibility of a supernatural source. In draft B he talks of a man's experience as being the foundation 'of all those notions which ever he shall have' [(2) 69]. But in the corresponding passage in the final *Essay* he refers instead to 'all those Notions, which ever he shall have naturally in this World' [II.i.24]. No doubt what he has in mind here is the possibility which is allowed in passing later on in the *Essay* that one 'may have from the immediate hand of GOD . . . Revelation . . . of new simple Ideas' [IV.xviii.3].

We have seen that Locke speaks of ideas both in the context of sensation and perception and in that of thought and the intellect. Though different, the two contexts are connected *via* his thesis that the contents of our thought, however abstract and removed from experience it may be, must in the end be derived from sensory experience:

All those sublime Thoughts, which towre above the Clouds, and reach as high as Heaven it self, take their Rise and Footing here: In all that great Extent wherein the mind wanders, in those remote Speculations, it may seem to be elevated with, it stirs not one jot beyond those Ideas, which Sense or Reflection, have offered. [II.i.24]

But though all the materials of knowledge, all ideas, come from experience we are not entirely passive. We are passive in that 'the Objects of our Senses, do, many of them, obtrude their particular Ideas upon our minds, whether we will or no' [II.i.25]. But we then go on actively to 'Enlarging, Compounding, and Abstracting' this sensory input [II.i.22].

By 'enlarging' and 'compounding' Locke has in mind two different processes by which we get from *simple* ideas to *complex* ideas. This distinction between the two sorts of idea is first made at II.ii.1. It qualifies the view that all our ideas come from sensation or reflection. We are restricted to experience for our simple ideas. But though the simple parts of a complex idea have to come from experience the complex idea itself need not. It can be made by the mind. 'When the Understanding is once stored with these simple Ideas [from sensation and reflection], it has the Power to repeat, compare, and unite them even to an almost infinite Variety, and so can make at Pleasure new complex Ideas' [II.ii.2]. Thus no one can 'fancy any Taste, which had never affected his Palate; or frame the Idea of a Scent, he had never smelt' [II.ii.2]. But one can conceive of a fruit smelling like this peach and tasting like this plum even though one has never had the good fortune to come across one.

In thinking in these terms of the composition of the complex out of the simple Locke was apparently 'accepting current fashion' [*Aaron* 111]. Descartes speaks of simple natures 'the cognition of which is so clear and so distinct that they cannot be analysed by the mind into others more distinctly known' and out of which all else is 'in some way compounded' [(1) 1.40-1]. Similarly Leibniz makes considerable use of the idea of 'primary concepts, by the combination of which the rest are formed'.[8] Locke's use of the idea of analysing complex thoughts and other mental items was evidently approved of by and endorsed in the practice of later philosophers such as George Berkeley (1685-1753), David Hume (1711-76), Étienne Condillac (1715-80), Thomas Reid (1710-96), John Stuart Mill (1806-73), and Ernst Mach (1838-1916).[9]

What Locke says about simple and complex ideas has an initial plausibility and straightforwardness which disappears on closer scrutiny. Sometimes the relationship between complex ideas and their parts is like the relationship between what the idea is an idea of and its physical parts. At these times the analysis of ideas into parts is analogous to physical dismemberment or division. Thus on one occasion Locke says that one might 'frame an Idea of the Legs, Arms, and Body of a Man, and join to this a Horse's Head and Neck' [II.xxxii.25]. Indeed Locke *defines* one of the sorts of complex ideas which he distinguishes as having a complexity of this sort. They (simple modes) are said to be 'different combinations of the same simple Idea . . . as a dozen, or score; which are nothing but the Ideas of so many distinct Unites added together' [II.xii.5]. Accordingly, and paralleling the fact that a dozen eggs is a collection of twelve eggs, Locke talks as though the idea of a dozen is twelve ideas of a single thing and not, as would be more plausible, one single idea of twelve things. But Locke does not always see the complexity of the idea of some physical thing as arising from the physical complexity of the thing. Sometimes he sees it as arising from the thing's having a number of properties. '[T]he Idea of the Sun, What is it, but an aggregate of those several simple Ideas, Bright, Hot, Roundish, having a constant regular motion, at a certain distance from us, and, perhaps, some other' [II.xxiii.6].

There is even a third approach to the decomposition of complex ideas into simple. This envisages it not as a sort of physical division, nor as a mere description or listing of properties, but as having to do with the definition of words or with the analysis of the concepts associated with those words. According to Locke the names of simple ideas are indefinable, for definition consists in splitting up the complex idea or concept with which a word is associated. 'And therefore a Definition, which is properly nothing but the shewing the meaning of one Word by several others not signifying each the same thing, can in the Names of simple Ideas have no place' [III.iv.7]. As we might expect, the meanings of the indefinable names of simple ideas are to be taught by presentation, by making a person 'actually have the Idea, that Word stands for' [III.xi.14]. As Locke explains,

> he that has not before received into his Mind, by the proper inlet, the simple Idea which any Word stands for, can never come to know the signification of that Word, by any other Words, or Sounds, whatsoever put together, according to any Rules of Definition. The only way is, by applying to his Senses the proper Object; and so producing that Idea in him, for which he has learn'd the name already. [III.iv.11]

An upshot of the distinction between simple and complex ideas is that we might have ideas which were not directly given in experience. This is possible so long as such ideas are complex and have simple parts that have been got directly from experience. But this does not mean that a complex idea *cannot* be got directly from experience and has always actually to be built up from experienced simples. Of a certain sort of complex idea (mixed modes) Locke says there are three ways in which we can get them. [II.xxii.9]. 'By Invention, or voluntary putting together of several simple Ideas in our own Minds', as when the inventor of etching had an idea of that process before it existed. We can get them 'by [someone] explaining the names of Actions we never saw'. And we can also get them 'By Experience and Observation of things themselves', as when by seeing two men wrestle or fence we get the complex ideas of wrestling or fencing. This is to say that often 'simple Ideas are observed to exist in several Combinations united together' [II.xii.1].

But are simple ideas ever 'observed to exist' singly and out of combination with others? Locke is not clear about this, and if there is a problem about the acquisition of ideas from experience it concerns not complex but simple ideas. He sometimes speaks as though experience is sufficient for our having simple ideas, as though the form our experience took was always of simples. 'Though the Qualities that affect our Senses, are, in the things themselves, so united and blended, that there is no separation, no distance between them; yet 'tis plain, the Ideas they produce in the Mind, enter by the Senses simple and unmixed' [II.ii.1]. On the other hand we have already seen that our experiences are sometimes complex and not always simple.

There are, furthermore, passages which say they are always complex and never simple. We are told, for example, that '*Existence* and *Unity*, are two . . . other Ideas, that are suggested to the Understanding, by every Object without, and every Idea within' [II.vii.7]. If then simple ideas do not come directly from experience, and are 'observed to exist in several combinations', how do they come? We get them by 'separating them from all other Ideas that accompany them in their real existence' [II.xii.1].

Book II begins straightforwardly enough with the thesis that ideas, the materials of knowledge, are derived from experience. But it does not go on to exhibit a very evident structure. It is a somewhat miscellaneous collection of chapters of basically two sorts. There are chapters about ideas in general. They distinguish various sorts of complex idea [xxii-xxv] and classify ideas into the true and the false, the clear and the obscure, and so-on [xxix-xxxii]. Then there are chapters about particular ideas such as 'solidity', 'personal identity', 'space' and 'time' and 'infinity'. Presumably one point of these chapters is to demonstrate by means of some particularly difficult cases just how all ideas are related to and grounded in experience. But it is clear too that these particular ideas have an intrinsic interest for Locke. Since we are concerned in this section with 'Ideas' generally we must look now at the first of these sets of chapters.

Besides the simple/complex classification Locke classifies ideas in five ways. They may be 'clear' or 'obscure' [xxix]; 'distinct' or 'confused' [xxix]; 'real' or 'fantastical' [xxx]; 'adequate' or 'inadequate' [xxxi]; and, finally, they may be 'true' or 'false' [xxxii]. As Locke himself makes plain, these categories were not invented by him. He says that '*Clear and distinct Ideas* are terms . . . familiar and frequent in Men's Mouths' [12]. Indeed the classification of ideas in these and other similar sorts of way was a commonplace in at any rate the second half of the seventeenth century. The notions of clarity, distinctness, and truth of ideas were quite central for Descartes [(1) 1.159-60, 237]. Spinoza divided ideas into the true and the false, the clear, distinct and the confused, and the adequate and the inadequate.[10] Arnauld and Nicole in *L'Art de Penser* (1662) and Arnauld in his *Traité des vraies et des fausses idées* (1683) saw them as being clear or obscure, distinct or confused, and perfect or imperfect.[11] While Leibniz' article 'Reflections on Knowledge, Truth, and Ideas' has the three categories of clarity and obscurity, distinctness and indistinctness, adequacy and inadequacy.[12] This article appeared in the scholarly Continental journal *Acta Eruditorum* in 1684 in response to Arnauld's book. Locke had both the journal and the book. It is quite possible he was inspired by them to discuss ideas in these sorts of terms. It seems to be about this time that the classifications make their way into the *Essay*. They first appear in draft C of 1686.

Locke's account of clarity and obscurity agrees pretty much with that of Descartes. We should understand these properties of ideas, he says, in terms of the clarity and obscurity of what we see. '[W]e give the name of *Obscure*, to that, which is not placed in a Light sufficient to discover minutely to us the Figure and Colours, which are observable in it, and which, in a better Light, would be discernible'. So ideas are obscure when they 'want any thing of that original Exactness, or have lost any of their first Freshness' [II.xxix.2]. Obscure ideas result from dull sense-organs, which are like wax which is too hard or too soft or which has a seal applied to it with insufficient force. In these circumstances an idea or 'print left by the Seal' will be obscure [II.xxix.3]. The properties of distinctness and confusedness are explained in the same chapter. Of them Locke says that

> As a *clear Idea* is that whereof the Mind has such a full and evident perception, as it does receive from an outward Object operating duly in a well-disposed Organ, so a *distinct Idea* is that wherein the Mind perceives a difference from all other; and a *confused Idea* is such an one, as is not sufficiently distinguishable from another, from which it ought to be different. [II.xxix.4]

But how, given this account of it, could ideas fail to be distinct? Surely ideas are as they are perceived to be. If the mind perceives two ideas to be different then they are different. If it perceives them to be the same then they are the same. How can we speak of one idea as being 'undistinguishable from another, from which it ought to be different'? The only way would seem to be for ideas to be different from themselves. Locke answers this problem by appealing to the names of ideas. We can call an

Locke

idea confused only when we refer to it as an idea of *such-and-such*, only when we specify it by name. '[W]ithout taking notice of such a reference of Ideas to distinct Names, as the signs of distinct Things, it will be hard to say what a confused Idea is' [II.xxix.10]. An idea is confused when it may as well be called by the name of some other idea. My idea of 'jealousy' is confused when it is no different from my idea of 'envy'. It is confused when 'the distinction, which was intended to be kept up by those different Names, is quite lost' [II.xxix.6]. There are, moreover, three ways in which an idea may be confused. First, an idea is confused when it is insufficiently detailed. '[H]e, that has an Idea made up of barely the simple ones of a Beast with Spots, has but a confused Idea of a Leopard, it not being thereby sufficiently distinguished from a Lynx, and several other sorts of Beasts that are spotted' [II.xxix.7]. Second, an idea may be confused because the ideas which make it up 'are so jumbled together, that it is not easily discernible, whether it more belongs to the Name that is given it, than to any other' [II.xxix.8]. Finally, we have confused ideas when we let the same name stand now for one idea, now for another.

When the pairs of properties of clarity and obscurity, distinctness and confusedness are both discussed in chapter xxix they are two quite different pairs. This is plain from what has just been said about them. But in the fourth edition of the *Essay* Locke speaks as though they were one and the same. To use his own terminology, he confuses them and fails to keep them distinct. In the 'Epistle to the Reader' he announces that he has made a certain terminological change in the new edition. He has, he says, 'in most places chose to put *determinate* or *determined*, instead of *clear* and *distinct*, as more likely to direct Men's thoughts to my meaning in this matter' [13].[13] The clear implication of this is that 'clear and distinct' is just one thing and not two that an idea might be. The intention to use the one word 'determined' underlines this. It is of passing interest to note that the explanation of 'determinateness' that Locke goes on to give identifies it with distinctness of the third kind.

How an idea fares with respect to Locke's other characterisations, whether it is real (or fantastical), adequate (or inadequate), true (or false) depends not only on whether it is simple or complex but also, if complex, on what sort of complex idea it is. As mentioned earlier, various sorts of these are distinguished and discussed. It turns out, furthermore, that the answer to Locke's initial question about the original, extent, and certainty of knowledge varies according to the adequacy, reality, and truth of the kind of complex idea involved. Discussion of these topics is of more immediate interest when (as in section 14) they take place against the background of some acquaintance with Locke's account of knowledge. We already have sufficient familiarity with ideas, the materials of knowledge, to be able to turn for a while to knowledge itself.

Notes

[1]   *A Free and Impartial Censure of the Platonick Philosophie* (1666), pp. 55-6.

[2]   The controversy began with Stillingfleet's *Discourse on the Vindication of the Trinity* (1696), and continued through Locke's *Letter* (1697), his *Reply to . . . Worcester's Answer . . . to his Letter* (1697) and his *Reply to . . . Worcester's Answer to his Second Letter* (1699).

[3]   For other criticisms see *Yolton* (1) 88-90.

[4]   See E.J. Ashworth, 'Descartes' theory of clear and distinct ideas', *Cartesian Studies*, ed. R.J. Butler (Blackwell, Oxford, 1972); R. McRae, ' "Idea" as a Philosophical Term in the Seventeenth Century', *Journal of the History of Ideas*, 26 (1965); J. Yolton, 'Ideas and Knowledge in Seventeenth-Century Philosophy', *Journal of the History of Philosophy*, 13(1975).

[5]   *Idea Philosophiae* (1631), p.95 (translated and quoted *Kenney* 162).

[6]   (2) 2. Sergeant (1662-1707), whose book was written against Locke, was a Catholic theologian and controversialist.

[7]   *Reflections upon a late Essay concerning Human Understanding* appended to *Christian Blessedness* (1690: reprinted Garland, New York and London, 1978), p.22.

[8]   *Leibniz: Philosophical Writings*, ed. G.H.R. Parkinson (Dent, London, 1973), p.11.

[9]   Respectively in *Principles of Human Knowledge* (1710), *A Treatise of Human Nature* (1739), *Traité des Sensations* (1754), *Essays on the Intellectual Powers of Man* (1785), *A System of Logic* (1843), and *The Analysis of Sensations* (1886).

[10]   *On the Improvement of the Understanding* (written 1662) and *The Ethics* (written 1675) in *Works of Spinoza*, vol. 1, trans. R.H.M. Elwes (Dover, New York, 1951). Benedict Spinoza (1632-77), Jewish philosopher and metaphysician, who lived in Holland.

[11]   *The Art of Thinking (Port-Royal Logic)*, trans. J. Dickoff, P.James (Bobbs-Merrill, Indianapolis, 1964), ch.9.

[12] In *Leibniz: Selections*, ed. P.P. Wiener (Charles Scribner's Sons, New York, 1951). Antoine Arnauld (1612-94) was a French theologian, mathematician and philosopher, known now for his objections to Descartes' *Meditations*. His *Traité* was written against Malebranche. Pierre Nicole (1625-95) was a French theologian and philosopher.

[13] Places where the change is made are II.xiii.14, III.x.23, IV.xii. 14 though not, interestingly enough, in II.xxix.

CHAPTER II

7 *Knowledge and how to get it*

Locke aims in the *Essay* to investigate the origin, certainty and extent of knowledge. We have seen him criticise and reject an account of the origination of knowledge according to which some of it is innate. He does not think any knowledge is innate. But nor does he think that any of it is derived from experience. What he does think is that the *materials* of knowledge, *ideas*, are derived from experience. How then is knowledge itself related to ideas? What is knowledge? It is defined at the beginning of Book IV, 'Of Knowledge and Opinion'. It is 'the perception of the connexion and agreement, or disagreement and repugnancy of any of our Ideas'. We know, for example, that 'the three Angles of a Triangle are equal to two right ones'. In knowing this what 'do we more but perceive, that Equality to two right ones, does necessarily agree to, and is inseparable from the three Angles of a Triangle'? We also know that 'White is not Black'. When we know this 'what do we else but perceive, that these two Ideas do not agree?'. It follows, of course, that where this perception is absent, 'though we many fancy, guess, or believe, yet we always come short of Knowledge' [IV.i.2].

'Disagreement' and 'repugnancy' seem to be two words for the same thing: incompatibility or inconsistency. The ideas of blackness and of whiteness disagree or are repugnant because a thing's being black is incompatible with its being white. There is an inconsistency in describing something as (uniformly) black and (uniformly) white. But are 'connexion' and 'agreement' two things or one? 'Agreement' sounds as though it is the opposite of 'disagreement'. If it is then, given that 'disagreement' is incompatibility or inconsistency, 'agreement' would be compatibility or consistency. But compatibility or consistency

is rather weaker than 'connexion'. There is compatibility
between something's being white and its being round: something could easily be both. But there is no 'connexion' between
a thing's being white and its being round. For there is an equal
compatibility between its being some other colour and its being
round. On the other hand, however, in giving the example of
the sum of the angles of a triangle Locke speaks as though
agreement is inseparability. This would make it the same as
connexion. Connexion itself should be understood to be something like entailment or implication. That there is a 'connexion'
between the ideas of being a triangle and having angles equal to
two right ones means that being a triangle entails or implies
having angles equal to two right ones.

Having defined knowledge in terms of perception of agreement and disagreement of ideas Locke proceeds to distinguish
four sorts of agreement and disagreement. These are 'identity or
diversity', 'relation', 'co-existence or necessary connexion' and
'real existence'. The first and third of these are merely special
and interesting cases of the second, 'relation'. Locke says that
they are 'truly nothing but Relations, yet . . . so peculiar . . .
that they deserve well to be considered as distinct Heads, and
not under Relation in general' [IV.i.7]. Thus *identity* and *diversity*, exemplified in 'white is white', or 'blue is not yellow', are
relations. So is *co-existence*, as when yellow colour and fixedness,
i.e. 'a power to remain in the fire unconsumed', are to be found
together in gold.

These four sorts of agreement between ideas are not quite so
straightforward as they might at first appear. For instance,
when the special cases of relation, the first and third of the four
sorts, are kept apart what remains under 'relation in general'?
Of course there will remain, as Locke says later on, 'any other
Relation' [IV.iii.18]. But what others are there? The example
that 'The Idea of a right-lined Triangle necessarily carries with
it an equality of its Angles to two right ones' [IV.iii.29] indicates
that 'equality' is another. But beyond this one it is not easy to
go. There is a problem, too, with the first special case of 'relation', namely 'identity and diversity'. When this is first introduced Locke says that 'the Ideas . . . White and Round, are the
very Ideas they are, and . . . not other Ideas . . . Red or Square'

[IV.i.4]. This seems to allow that 'white' and 'round' are as diverse as 'round' and 'square' are. But though whiteness and roundness certainly are two *different* qualities they are not actually *incompatible*. Yet this is what diverse or non-identical ideas later seem to be [IV.vii.4].

'Relation' and 'identity' are not the only kinds of 'agreement' between ideas that present difficulties. The other two do also. Locke speaks of 'co-existence *or* necessary connexion'. Are these meant to be synonyms? Sometimes they seem to be [IV.i.3, vii.5]. If they are, then to say that the various properties of gold 'co-exist' would be to say not merely that they are all in fact found together, but that they necessarily are. It would be to say, for example, that gold *has* to be malleable. But at other times 'co-existence' seems to be different from and weaker than 'necessary connexion' [IV.i.6]. To say that the properties of gold 'co-exist' would now be to say merely that gold as it happens is malleable. There is a further difficulty about 'co-existence'. It shares this with the fourth sort of 'agreement', that of 'real existence'. They are both supposed to be cases of agreement *between ideas*. But are they really? Whether it has any necessity about it or not the malleability of gold is surely not a matter of the co-existence of *ideas*. It is a matter of the co-existence of qualities of pieces of metal in the material world. 'Real existence', as exemplified in the proposition that 'God is', is similarly officially supposed to be a matter of agreement of *ideas*. But Locke does not in fact speak of it as though it did concern the agreement of an idea, e.g. the idea of God, with some other idea. He treats it as though it concerned the agreement of an idea with 'actual real Existence', with some part of the world.

These difficulties concerning the four sorts of agreement and disagreement of ideas appear only at a closer look. Let us avoid them, even if only for the moment, by withdrawing to a position from which Locke is seen to be saying simply that knowledge is a matter of perceiving connexions between ideas. Viewed from this position knowledge results from the fact that 'In some of our Ideas there are certain Relations, Habitudes, and Connexions, so visibly included in the Nature of the Ideas themselves, that we cannot conceive them separable from them, by any Power whatsoever. And in these only, we are capable of certain and universal Knowledge' [IV.iii.29].

We have yet to see in detail how Locke assesses the extent of knowledge. But something may already occur to us about the above analysis. Does it not make a quite drastic restriction on the extent of knowledge? It seems plausible to think that knowledge of the equality of the external angles of a triangle to its two internal opposite angles is based on perception of a connexion between the ideas of a triangle and of its various angles. At least so long as we were not accepting the information on the say-so of some teacher it would seem to be based on this perception. But what of the knowledge that iron rusts when left out in the rain? What of the knowledge that gold is malleable and pencil lead not? This is surely *not* based on perception of any connexion between ideas. It is based rather on observation, experience, and informal experiment. But if so, if such cases are not based on the perception of agreement between ideas, then the terms of Locke's analysis rule out these everyday cases as cases of knowledge at all. Locke himself accepts this. He recognises there are cases, such as those mentioned above, where there is 'a want of a discoverable Connection between those Ideas which we have'. There are, that is, cases where we are 'left only to Observation and Experiment' [IV.iii.28]. Having recognised this he says, consistently with his definition of knowledge, that they do not constitute 'universal and certain Knowledge'. They are, rather, cases of 'Faith, or Opinion' [IV.ii.14]. At first sight it may seem puzzling that Locke should restrict 'knowledge' in this way. But, as we shall be in a position to see in section 9, his distinction between 'knowledge' and 'opinion' both acknowledges an earlier Aristotelian distinction and anticipates one which would be generally accepted today.

Against the background of this definition of knowledge, three 'degrees' or grades of knowledge are distinguished. The first of these is *intuitive*. Knowledge is of this 'degree' when 'the Mind perceives the Agreement or Disagreement of two Ideas immediately by themselves, without the intervention of any other'. An instance would be when 'the Mind perceives at the first sight of the Ideas together . . . without the intervention of any other Idea' that 'a Circle is not a Triangle' [IV.ii.1].

This notion of *intuition* connects Locke's positive account of knowledge with his negative criticism of innate knowledge in Book I. It will be remembered that Locke objected to the idea that their innateness would satisfactorily explain why certain truths seemed obvious. At the time he promised to give an alternative account of self-evidence, one which did not rely on the postulation of innateness. What he says about *intuition* fulfills that promise. According to his alternative view a proposition will be self-evident when the ideas in it are such that the mind can directly perceive a connexion between them. A proposition's being such that its constituent ideas are immediately connected is, unlike its being innate, of course an internal fact about it. Locke's explanation makes self-evidence a property of propositions in themselves and not a merely external property about propositions in relation to our minds.

Knowledge of the second 'degree' or grade is *demonstrative*. Here we perceive the agreement of ideas, not immediately, but by a chain of intermediate ideas. At each step of this chain there is an intuitive perception of immediate agreement. One cannot 'by an immediate view and comparing them' know that the three angles of a triangle are equal to two right angles. In this case the mind needs to 'find out some other Angles, to which the three Angles of a Triangle have an Equality; and finding those equal to two right ones, comes to know their Equality to two right ones' [IV.ii.2]. Locke is right about this. It is *not* immediately obvious that the angles of a triangle equal two right ones. But he gives no detail about the example. However some of the requisite intermediate ideas, or 'proofs' [IV.ii.3], or 'mediums' [IV.xvii.15] come to mind if one imagines a line through the apex of a triangle parallel to its base. This produces, on the line, two other angles adjacent to the apex angle of the triangle. Together with the apex angle these are angles on a straight line and so obviously equal two right angles. It is now evident, furthermore, that one of these two further angles equals one of the base angles of the triangle. The other similarly equals the other base angle. It is now evident that, since the angles on the apex-line equal two right angles, the angles of the triangle equal two right-angles.

Knowledge of the third 'degree' is 'sensitive knowledge'. This is knowledge of 'the existence of particular external Objects, by that perception and Consciousness we have of the actual entrance of Ideas from them' [IV.ii.14]. Discussion of it may be left till section 15.

It is generally agreed that what Locke says about intuition and demonstration has obvious and close affinities with Descartes' doctrine about the way in which knowledge is to be acquired.[1] Descartes was much impressed by the fact that of all the sciences 'Arithmetic and Geometry alone are free from any taint of falsity or uncertainty' [(1) 1.4]. He explained how knowledge is acquired in those sciences in terms of two 'mental operations', *intuition* and *deduction*, by which we are able 'wholly without fear of illusion to arrive at knowledge'. What he says about 'intuition' and 'deduction' is echoed by what Locke says about 'intuition' and 'demonstration'. There are parallels also in detail about the second sort of knowledge. In a long deduction, Locke says, 'the Memory does not always so readily and exactly retain' the intuitive perception of each step. As a result demonstrative knowledge 'is more imperfect than intuitive Knowledge and Men embrace often Falshoods for Demonstrations'. Similarly Descartes attributes some uncertainty about a demonstrative conclusion to the weakness of memory. We cannot simultaneously have an intuitive grasp of all the steps in a proof. We have to rely on a memory of our intuitions of the earlier ones [(1) 1.34]. Though it is clear that there is an affinity between Locke and Descartes on these matters the historical facts about how it arises are not so clear. Descartes' *Rules for the Direction of the Mind*, in which he put forward these ideas was not published until 1701, eleven years after the publication of the *Essay*. But copies of it had circulated for years before. So it has been suggested that when Locke was in France (1675-9) or Holland (1683-9) he saw a copy. Or perhaps he assimilated its content in the course of discussion with Descartes' followers.

We have noted the impression that arithmetic and geometry made on Descartes in that they, of all the sciences, seemed free from falsity and uncertainty. So strong was it that he concluded that the method of intuition and demonstration which they embodied was *the* method to be used in any search for knowledge:

Those long chains of reasoning, simple and easy as they are, of which geometricians make use in order to arrive at the most difficult demonstrations, had caused me to imagine that all those things which fall under the cognizance of man might very likely be mutually related in the same fashion; and that, provided . . . [we follow the same method] there can be nothing so remote that we cannot reach it, nor so recondite that we cannot discover it. [(1) 1.92]

We shall see that Locke did not share Descartes' conviction about the universal applicability of this method. 'Intuition' and 'demonstration' are, after all, degrees of *knowledge*, and we have already seen that Locke speaks of 'opinion' as well as of 'knowledge'. Nevertheless he was sure that its range was not restricted to mathematics. 'It has been generally taken for granted, that Mathematicks alone are capable of demonstrative certainty . . . [but this is] as I imagine, not the privilege of the Ideas of Number, Extension, and Figure alone' [IV.ii.9]. One of these further areas where, in Locke's view, we could have 'demonstrative certainty' is that of morality. This perhaps surprising suggestion that it could be possible to 'place Morality among the Sciences capable of Demonstration' [IV.iii.18], a suggestion some of whose detail will be looked at in section 15, raises a number of general questions. Why is it that we have knowledge in some areas and not in others? What would allow us to get knowledge in new areas? How are we to extend and improve our knowledge?

A whole chapter on 'The Improvement of our Knowledge' [IV.xii] addresses itself to the last of these questions. In it Locke contrasts his own view of the matter with another which he rejects:

But since . . . Knowledge . . . depends only upon the perception, we have, of the Agreement, or Disagreement of our Ideas, the way to improve our Knowledge, is not, I am sure, blindly, and with an implicit Faith, to receive and swallow Principles; but is, I think, to get and fix in our Minds clear, distinct, and complete Ideas . . . . And thus, perhaps, without any other Principles, but barely considering those Ideas, and by comparing them one with another, finding their Agreement, and Disagreement, and their several Relations and Habitudes; we shall get more true and clear Knowledge, by the conduct of this one Rule, than by taking up Principles, and thereby putting our Minds into the disposal of others. [IV.xii.6; also 15]

This passage opposes Locke's own idea about the 'improvement' of knowledge to another which has to do with 'taking up Principles'. This other is in fact the Scholastic account of the development and advancement of demonstrative knowledge or *scientia* which was outlined in section 5. Before going further we must now look in detail at this Scholastic account and at Locke's objections to it.

Notes

[1] For dissenting views see Thomas O'Kelley, 'Locke's doctrine of intuition was not borrowed from Descartes', *Philosophy*, 46 (1971); H.A.S. Schankula, 'Locke, Descartes, and the Science of Nature', *Journal of the History of Ideas*, 41 (1980).

8 Aristotelian Demonstration rejected

We learnt a little about the Aristotelian or Scholastic theory of *scientia* or scientific knowledge in section 5. We shall look at it here in more detail.

Locke's own account of the theory is rather brief. After all, he says, it was 'the common received Opinion amongst Men of Letters'. He says little more than that these men of 'the Schools', the Scholastics of the time, held 'that Maxims were the foundations of all Knowledge; and that the Sciences were each of them built upon certain *praecognita*, from whence the Understanding was to take its rise, and by which it was to conduct it self, in its enquiries into the matters belonging to that Science' [IV.xii.1; also vii.8, 10,11].

Two different sources have been drawn on for the following less brief account (and for accounts in later sections of other Scholastic doctrines). First there are the original Aristotelian texts (together with modern commentaries on these). Then there are seventeenth-century logic texts in which Aristotelian doctrines are set forth in a rather uncritical and stylised way. The product of combining these two kinds of source is bound to be an idealisation. Aristotle's doctrines had undergone modification and addition by the seventeenth century. For instance we saw in section 5 that the theory of scientific knowledge, the particular doctrine that concerns us in this section, became associated with a non-Aristotelian doctrine of innateness.

Section 5 warned that we must not expect this theory, which originates in the first book of Aristotle's *Posterior Analytics*, to capture or fit what we today mean by 'science', or 'knowledge'. One big difference is that knowledge as defined by it is of what is necessary and cannot be otherwise. There can be no knowledge, strictly speaking, of things that are so but which may have been otherwise. 'Opinion', not knowledge, has to do with contingent facts of this sort. Another significant feature is that the theory partly explains the nature of man. Man's rationality, which is what differentiates him from other animals, is most properly exercised in the acquisition of *scientia*. *Scientia* is a fit aim for his intellectual endeavours.

Scientia, then, concerns what is necessary. But to know that something must be so and cannot be otherwise is to give a satisfactory demonstration of it. Furthermore, to give a demonstration of something is, the theory explains, to derive it by means of a *syllogistic* argument from certain *axioms* or *first principles*. In order for these first principles to serve as satisfactory starting points they need to be true. If they were not we could hardly see why what we derive from them must be true. They need also to be 'primary and indemonstrable' [71b27]. If they were not then a demonstration would be required of *them*. Finally they need to be 'the causes of . . . , better known than . . . , and prior to' the conclusion we establish on their basis [71b 29-30]. If they were not, then the proper order of demonstration and explanation would have been reversed. Such axioms or first principles have gone by various names. Locke refers to them both by the Greek phrase 'koinai ennoi' (common notions) and by a Latin word, 'praecognita' [I.ii.1, IV. xii. 1]. The first of these does not come from Aristotle but from the slightly later *Elements of Geometry* of Euclid. The second is from Latin translations of Aristotle and is descriptive of the characteristics of a satisfactory starting point.

The starting points of scientific knowledge are of two sorts. First there are things that have to be known if anything at all is to be known. Aristotle gives as examples the law of non-contradiction (that nothing can both be and not be), the law of the excluded middle (that a thing either is or is not), and the proposition that if equals are taken from equals then equals remain. This third example turned up later as one of Euclid's 'common notions'. The second sort of starting point is special to the subject matter under consideration. In effect it picks that subject matter out and defines it. As the English word 'science' might lead us to expect, *scientia* falls into various bodies of knowledge, or sciences. What distinguishes them from each other is that they deal with different subject matters. Each science has to do with its own *genus* or 'kind' which is divided into various species. Geometry deals with *plane figures* such as *triangles* and *squares*. Similarly biology has as its subject the genus *animal*, a genus which falls into various species such as *dog* or *horse*. Each science needs to be prefaced by an account or definition of the genus and the various species with which it deals.

Where does our knowledge of the first principles of all other knowledge come from? It can hardly be got by reason and demonstration. So is it acquired in some other way, or is it innate? According to Aristotle it is not innate but is acquired, ultimately from sense-experience, by means of a faculty of 'intellectual intuition'. Experience of particular instances of some first principle leads us to grasp its general truth intellectually. Though Aristotle himself did not appeal to innateness in his account of the development and structure of knowledge we have seen that some of his followers did. The three examples of Aristotelian axioms cited at the beginning of the last paragraph are precisely Locke's examples of speculative principles held by some to be innate. But other scholastics kept closer to the master. The *praecognita* in *Tractatus de Demonstratione* (1651) of the Oxford logician John Flavel (1596-1617) are not innate [*Kenney* 165]. Equally, those of Sergeant's *Method to Science* have an obviousness that is not derived from their being innate [(1) 131].

Why are the first principles which are peculiar and special to each science *definitions?* Scientific knowledge is knowledge that something must be so and cannot be otherwise. But to see *that* something is so and cannot be otherwise is to see *why* it is so. And to see why it is so is to understand its causes. A cause is that from which something comes and thus that which explains why it is so and not otherwise. Just as the starting points of a scientific demonstration must be the 'cause' of the conclusion so what these premises record must be the cause of what is being demonstrated and explained. So to have scientific knowledge of some fact is to have knowledge of its causes.

Now according to Aristotle there are four sorts of cause: *material, formal, final,* and *efficient*. The bronze of a statue or the silver of a bowl are their material causes. The human shape of the statue and the roundness of the bowl are their formal causes.

Their final causes are the purposes for which they were made. Finally, the people who made the statue and the bowl are their efficient causes. To see why some first principles are definitions we must concentrate on formal causality.

We have just seen that the *form* (or *nature* or *essence*) of something is at least one sort of reason or cause for it. To ask 'What is an eclipse?' is to ask 'What is the reason for or cause of an eclipse?' But what captures the form or nature of a kind or species of thing is, of course, nothing other than the definition of that species. '[D]efinition reveals essential nature' [91a1]. Hence the definitions with which each science is prefaced provide the means to acquire knowledge of the reasons or causes for certain facts. Which facts are these? They must of course be facts which are necessary and which cannot be otherwise. But in order to see just which these are we must investigate the structure of a definition. We must see in what way they capture the forms or natures of species. This involves us with the doctrine of the 'predicables' as given in Aristotle's *Topics, Metaphysics,* and *Posterior Analytics.*

Aristotelian definitions are what are called *real* rather than merely *nominal* [*Burgersdijck* 2.3; *Spencer* 184 f.]. A nominal definition gives us a superficial description of the things to which a word applies. To say that men live in houses and wear clothes or that universities are places where people listen to others talking, is to give a merely nominal description of these things. A real definition, however, is meant to afford insight into what something really or essentially is. It captures the essence or essential attributes by giving the *genus* to which that kind or *species* of things belongs and the *differentia* which makes it differ from other species and makes it the species that it is. *Triangles* belong to the genus *plane figure* and are differentiated from other species in that genus by *having three sides.* A definition of a species will obviously not include attributes which may or may not belong to things of that species. It will not include attributes which do not belong permanently to them. These are called *accidents* or *separable accidents.* It is an accident of a particular triangle that its sides are the length they happen to be. So the essential definition of a triangle will not include having sides of any particular length.

We have noted that along with principles which are common to all the sciences these real definitions of the essences of things are arrived at on the basis of sense-experience by means of intellectual intuition. When one has for some time dealt with plane figures of various sorts and become familiar with them it is possible for one to come to see that what is triangular is essentially a plane figure of three sides. Aristotle uses the word 'induction' in this connexion. A universal truth is elicited from or discerned in our experience of a number of particulars.

Besides the essence of a species or kind (given by the genus and the differentia) and the separable accidents there are also *properties* or *inseparable accidents*. Unlike separable accidents these are permanent and universal attributes of members of a species. Triangles, for example, all permanently have angles equal to two right angles. But having angles of this size is no part of the essence or definition of a triangle. The complete essence of a triangle is to be a three-sided plane figure. But there is no doubt however that though having angles equal to two right-angles is not part of the essence of a triangle it is *because* triangles *are* three-sided plane figures that they *do* have angles of this size. The essence of a species accounts for the properties or inseparable accidents of that species. A real definition gives us the means to arrive at a species' properties. Indeed, facts about what are the properties of a given species are exactly the facts that a science, with its initial definitions, is meant to give us knowledge of. Science is knowledge of what is necessarily the case and of why it is so. The properties of a species necessarily belong to things of that kind, and the essence or definition of that species is the cause or reason for their having those properties. So one has acquired scientific knowledge when one has a series of syllogisms which, on the basis of definitions and other first principles, demonstrate that the properties or inseparable accidents of the species in question must belong to it. Just as essences give rise to those properties so definitions of those essences, when used as premisses, give rise to conclusions about those properties.

Locke, we saw, described this account as a 'common received Opinion'. Lee thought this an exaggeration. According to him, 'the Men of Letters he [Locke] means, have no such wild

Conceipts concerning the Influence of the common Principles of
Reason; for I never met with one that was so fond of them, as to
own, that all the Knowledge he pretended to in . . . any . . .
Science, was the sole Product of those Maxims' [294]. But Lee
was writing in 1702. In earlier years the Aristotelian idea that
knowledge is a matter of syllogistically deriving conclusions
from first principles and definitions certainly had its supporters.
It is easy enough to find its various parts being taken for granted
in the seventeenth century. The following fairly random collection of quotations makes this clear. Richard Crakanthorpe
(1567-1624) explains in his *Logicae Libri Quinque* (1622) that in
order to learn one cannot ignore undemonstrable axioms or
principles such as that 'anything . . . exists or does not exist' or
'it is impossible for [anything] . . . at one and the same time to
be the same and not the same' [*Howell* 23]. Spencer says that for
a man to know is for him to 'know one thing lesse known, by the
light and reflection of another thing, that is better knowne' [8].
Glanvill refers to 'foundation-*Propositions*', such as that 'it is
impossible for the same thing to be, and not to be'. These are
'the very *Essentials* of Rationality' and from them new conclusions are to be deduced [(1) 97-8]. Norris expounds the same
general view about the structure of knowledge:

> whatever we know, we may be said to know it either as a *Principle*, or as a
> *Conclusion*. As a Principle that has an internal Evidence, and shines as we
> say by its own light . . . or as a conclusion, which being not evident of it self,
> must be render'd so by the help of an external Light let in upon it.
> [2.145-6]

The doctrine of *scientia* found one of its fullest seventeenth-
century expressions in Sergeant's *Method to Science*. He explains
that 'the Deducing Evidently New Knowledges out of Antecedent ones' is part of 'our very *Essence* and *Rational Nature*'. The
way to acquire knowledge, 'the method to science', consists of
these steps:

> our Notions being Clear'd, First Principles establish'd, the true Form of a
> Syllogism manifested, Proper Middle Terms found, and the Necessity of
> the Consequence evidenced; all those Conclusions may be Deduced with
> *Demonstrative Evidence*, which ly within our Ken, or which we can have
> occasion to enquire after. [Preface]

Sergeant's defence of the theory in 1696 came after some decades of attack on it. In the 1660s Sprat had referred disparagingly to the attempts of the 'Schole-men' to spread knowledge 'by insisting altogether on established *Axioms*' and on the 'inferring one thing from another' [17]. He was critical of their method of enquiry which was to begin 'with some general Definitions'. But earlier attacks like those of Sprat are nothing like so systematic or detailed as the later ones of Locke.

Before looking at these we should recall the following features of the theory of *scientia*. A belief which is not acquired in the way the theory specifies cannot count as knowledge. Unless we have syllogistically shown from first principles and definitions that something must be so and cannot be otherwise then we do not have knowledge of it. At best we have 'opinion'. Furthermore, the way to acquire knowledge, to extend and develop it, is to make new derivations of this kind. Finally, the theory includes the idea that man's rationality, which is part of his very essence, is most properly expressed in the acquisition of *scientia*. As Sergeant puts it, 'the Deducing Evidently New Knowledges out of Antecedent ones' is part of 'our very *Essence* and *Rational Nature*'.

Locke's criticisms of this theory occur at various places in the *Essay* and touch it at almost every point. According to the theory all knowledge rests on certain primary and undemonstrable axioms or principles. We must have knowledge of these before anything else can be known. We have seen that in Book I Locke argues against the version of this theory according to which our knowledge of these principles is innate. He points out, for example, that many more propositions are obvious than are (officially) innate. This casts doubt on the use of innateness to explain obviousness. He repeats essentially this point against versions of the theory which, like Norris's, give some other account of this primary knowledge, or which remain silent on the issue. He observes that the particular propositions which are actually picked out as being basic *praecognita* are not the only ones which are undemonstrable and obvious in themselves. 'A man is not a horse' and 'Red is not Blew' are merely two more amongst many. 'It is not therefore alone to these two general Propositions, *Whatsoever is is*; and, *It is impossible for the same Thing to be, and not to be,* that this Self-evidence belongs by any peculiar right' [IV.vii.4].

These examples show that it is simply false that everything we know is either a Scholastic maxim or is derived from such maxims. They show also that there is no reason to focus on rather general propositions of this sort and to suppose they have particular significance. Locke does believe, we know, that knowledge may be intuitive or may be demonstrative. Accordingly he can agree with the Scholastics that everything we know is either known in itself (intuitively) or is derived from something known in itself (demonstratively). But he need not and does not agree that this derivation is always and in all cases from general maxims or principles. He need not agree either that anything that is undemonstrated and intuitively known is some such general maxim. Propositions of many sorts are obvious in themselves and need no derivation from others. Ranging from 'Whatever is, is' to 'the idea of white is the idea of white' they range from the portentous to the trivial. This is an embarrassment to those who think that undemonstrable propositions must have a special status at the foundation of our knowledge. It is even more of an embarrassment if one also thinks that our knowledge of them requires them to be innate. From Locke's point of view, however, this multiplicity and variety is unsurprising and without significance. For him the obviousness of a proposition has to do with a feature of the proposition itself. It does not have to do with God's having chosen to make the proposition innate. It simply has to do with our being able to see that one idea is the idea that it is and not any other. So the triviality that 'the Idea of White, is the Idea of White, and not the Idea of Blue' [IV.vii.4] is on a footing quite equal with the 'general maxim' that 'Whatsoever is, is'. It can be known without the help of prior knowledge of that maxim. Indeed as anti-Scholastics such as Bacon [4.25, 50, 97, 111, 411] and Webster [34] had already argued, it could even be said that the order of priority amongst these two propositions needs reversing. We certainly do not need to know that 'Whatever is, is' before we can know that 'blue is blue'. On the contrary, it is plausible to suppose that we know the particular truths first and then, by generalising, arrive at the more abstract ones, the so-called maxims [IV.vii.4, 9-10, xii.3].

According to the theory of demonstration, maxims or principles are not the only things required for the derivation of *scientia*. Definitions of the species under consideration are also required. In Book III, 'Of Words', Locke frequently attacks the idea of real definition that is involved here. What he says often takes the form of a claim that the essences of things are not 'real' but are the products of human convention. In reading it it must be borne in mind that, as will be clear in section 12, Locke has his own account of 'real essence' and so does not completely reject the idea out of hand. He simply rejects the Scholastic account associated with the theory of real definition.

Locke argues against that theory that if there were something that men really are, some formula definitive of the nature of man, it would not be possible that different people give different meanings to the word 'man.' 'It could not possibly be, that the abstract Idea, to which the name *Man* is given, should be different in several Men, if it were of Nature's making; and that to one it should be *Animal rationale* [rational animal], and to another *Animal implume bipes latis unguibus*, [featherless wide-nailed biped]' [III.vi.26]. Locke does not face the suggestion that one of these definitions could still be correct. But it is easy to see what his attitude towards it would be. He tells of an argument between 'learned and ingenious Physicians' whether 'Liquor passed through the Filaments of the Nerves'. Locke, with a predisposition to suspect 'that the greatest part of Disputes were more about the signification of Words', suggested they 'examine and establish amongst them, what the Word *Liquor* signified'. They found that each 'made it a sign of a different complex Idea', that 'the Main of their Dispute was about the signification of that Term' and so was 'not worth the contending about' [III.ix.16]. But there is more to the idea of real definition than Locke allows. Questions of classification and definition are *not* purely conventional and arbitrary. One of his examples of a trivial dispute is 'Whether a Bat were a Bird, or no' [III.xi.7]. Yet when John Ray (1627-1705), the naturalist, decided, but three years after the publication of the *Essay* as it happens, that a bat is not a bird he 'made an important step towards the formulation of the concept mammal'.[1]

The theory of *scientia* also holds that the derivation of all our fresh knowledge from *praecognita* and definitions is carried on in syllogistic form. Indeed just as reason was part of the essence of man so the syllogism was supposed to be the very form of that rationality itself. Now Locke is not against the use of reason as such. There is great need of it 'both for the enlargement of our Knowledge, and regulating our Assent' [IV.xvii.2]. He even goes so far as to allow that 'the greatest part of our Knowledge depends upon Deductions' [IV.xvii.2]. What he is against, however, is the idea that reason is completely embodied in and expressed by the syllogism. He doubts 'whether *Syllogism*, as is generally thought, be the proper instrument of [reason], and the usefullest way of exercising this Faculty' [IV.xvii.4]. If one has the vague idea that syllogisms are simply arguments or pieces of reasoning laid out in some rather formal manner, what Locke says here will seem puzzling. It will look as though he is in effect suggesting that reasoning is not the best exercise of our faculty of reason. But a glance at any recent logic text-book which contains a section on 'Traditional Logic' will show that there is a highly detailed and well-worked out *theory* of the syllogism.[2] Though syllogisms come in a variety of forms there are quite strict and clear rules, laid down by Aristotle in the *Prior Analytics* and *De Interpretatione*, as to what does and what does not count as one. In a memorable piece of sarcasm about the importance the Scholastics gave to the syllogism Locke dryly remarks that God 'has not been so sparing to Men to make them barely two-legged Creatures, and left it to *Aristotle* to make them Rational' [IV.xvii.4].

Locke's objections to the idea that human reason is completely embodied in the syllogism and must properly take that form are made on more than one front. First he argues that reasoning does not always take this form. Then he argues that arguments of this form are sometimes more confusing than illuminating. Thus he suggests to begin with that our faculty of reason can be exercised in a number of ways [IV.xvii. 2-3]. We may use it to discover or invent a proof or argument. We may use it to set out that argument in a perspicuous fashion. Our reason is used also in following and grasping the point of the various steps and conclusion of an argument which someone else presents. The syllogism, however, is relevant only to the third of these exercises of the faculty of reason. Moreover it is not necessary even here: An argument does not even have to approximate to standard syllogistic form for it to be followed. Observation shows that many people do not in fact reason syllogistically. Syllogistic form cannot be *the* form of reason. 'He that will look into many parts of Asia and America, will find Men reason there . . . who yet never heard of a Syllogism, nor can reduce any one Argument to those Forms: and I believe scarce any one ever makes Syllogisms in reasoning within himself' [IV.xvii.4].

This shows that, as a matter of psychological fact, people do not, in their informal thinking and ruminating, follow syllogistic patterns. But perhaps this is not what Locke needs to show. For the idea that human reason is essentially syllogistical could be interpreted as the idea that any argument *can* explicitly and with illumination be put into this form. This is certainly the way Lee interprets it. For he answers that despite what Locke says, a person's reasoning may nevertheless 'amount to' a syllogism. Even people in Asia and America 'discourse Syllogistically whether they know it or not' [314]. Locke of course would concede that arguments *can*, at least often, be put into syllogistic form. But he would insist that people do not find it the most useful or proper form. They do not reason syllogistically when they first reach a conclusion. They do not present syllogisms when trying to convince others. Sometimes indeed some syllogistic reasoning will be accepted only *after* the acceptance of some related non-syllogistic reasoning. Similarly, putting an argument into this form may make it more difficult to follow. These points, made in rapid succession in IV.xvii.4, do not exhaust Locke's passionate outburst against the syllogism. He suggests also that there is no reason to think that the syllogistic form has any necessary connexion with the laying bare of fallacies. On the contrary, perhaps 'these artificial Methods of reasoning [are] more adapted [than others] to catch and intangle the Mind'.

According to Aristotle, knowledge, or *scientia*, is arrived at on the basis of syllogisms whose premisses are 'true and primary' [*Topics* 100a28], necessarily and undoubtedly true. If we began with premisses which are merely probable in being about things which may have been otherwise, or about opinions which are merely 'generally accepted' [*Topics* 100a31] then all we can have is 'opinion' or 'belief'. Now Locke's strictures on the syllogism sometimes have in mind its use in connexion with this *dialectical* establishment of matters of opinion rather than with the *demonstrative* attainment of knowledge. This is so when in making the point that the syllogism is perhaps better suited to confuse than to enlighten he says that 'Syllogism has been thought more proper for the attaining Victory in dispute, than for the Discovery or Confirmation of Truth, in fair Enquiries' [IV.xvii.4]. It is so also when he says that the syllogism is of even less use 'in Probabilities' than in knowledge, and refers to the idea of 'topical Argument' [IV.xvii.5].

The dialectical use of the syllogism is the subject of Aristotle's *Topics*. A feature of life in classical Greece was public argument and competitive debate. The *Topics* is effectively a handbook for the participants, the 'questioner' and the 'answerer', in such debates. Much of it consists of a discussion of *topoi* (hence the name of the book), 'places' or 'commonplaces' of argument. The idea of a *topos* survives today in the word 'commonplace' and in the phrase 'In the first/second/third place . . . ' round which people often structure their arguments. In effect *topoi* were recommended standard moves which might be made, either constructively or destructively, in any argument. One might, for example, try to counter an opponent by distinguishing what one actually meant from what the opponent tried to refute. The *Topics* also contains directions, some of them less than honest, to be followed in arguments by both participants. For example, 'It is a good rule also, occasionally to bring an objection against oneself: for answerers are put off their guard against those who appear to be arguing impartially' [156b 18-20].

This feature of classical Greek life, together with Aristotle's written contribution to it, became part of the Scholastic tradition. Formal disputations carried on in syllogistic form were a significant part of intellectual and academic life in the seventeenth century. For example university students for the Bachelor's degree had to take part in them, for Aristotle had

said they might be used 'for the sake of training and examination' [159a25] in arguing. But along with other aspects of
that tradition they increasingly came under attack. From
Bacon [4.24, 25, 50, 411] and Descartes [(1) 1.124]
onwards to Webster [33, 38, 67, 92] and Hooke scorn was poured
on the litigious and quarrelsome 'philosophy of discourse and
disputation' [*Hooke* 3]. Sprat inveighs against 'mens spending
the strength of their thoughts about *Disputes*' [341; also 17,
326-7, 332]. Glanvill says ' '*Tis no good fishing* for Verity *in
troubled waters* . . . the precipitancy of *disputation*, and the stir and
noise of Passions, that usually attend it; must needs be pre-
judicial to Verity' [(1) 164-5; also 159].

We have already noted two passages in which Locke adds his
weight to these complaints about the disputation and its instrument, the dialectical syllogism. In others he criticises 'Schoolmen', those 'learned Disputants' or 'all-knowing Doctors',
whose 'artificial Ignorance and learned Gibberish, [has] pre-
vailed mightily in these last Ages'. He taxes them with having
found 'no easier way to that pitch of Authority and Dominion
they have attained, than by amusing the Men of Business, and
Ignorant, with hard Words, or imploying the Ingenious and
Idle in intricate Disputes, about unintelligible Terms, and
holding them perpetually entangled in that endless Labyrinth'
[III.x.6ff.]. His attitude towards the whole business is summed
up in the forthright advice he gives parents 'not to let your son
be bred up in the art and formality of disputing . . . unless,
instead of an able man, you desire to have him an insignificant
wrangler . . . questioning every thing, and thinking there is no
such thing as truth to be sought, but only victory, in disputing
[(5) 9.178].[3]

There is one final point which must be made about the theory
of scientific demonstration and Locke's criticisms of it. There is
a difference between an account of the way new knowledge
should be discovered and developed, and one of the way knowledge already possessed by some people should be taught or
communicated to others. Even if Locke himself had not drawn
attention to this distinction we would in any case have known
that his interest in the Scholastic theory concerned its supposedly being an account of the first sort. For we saw at the end

of the last section that what he wants to substitute for the theory is his own view about the development and acquisition of knowledge. Accordingly we find him conceding that though the Scholastic method of demonstration from first principles might help in 'teaching Sciences so far as they are advanced' it is 'not of use to help Men forwards in the Advancement of Sciences, or new Discoveries of yet unknown Truths':

> Would those who . . . think no Step can be made in Knowledge without the support of an *Axiom*, no Stone laid in the building of the Sciences without a general *Maxim*, but distinguish between the Method of acquiring Knowledge, and of communicating it; between the Method of raising any Science, and that of teaching it to others as far as it is advanced, they would see that those general *Maxims* were not the foundations on which the first Discoverers raised their admirable Structures, nor the Keys that unlocked and opened those Secrets of Knowledge. Though afterwards, when Schools were erected, and Sciences had their Professors to teach what others had found out, they often made use of *Maxims*. [IV.vii.11]

Locke was not the first to think that syllogistically deriving conclusions from first principles provides only a method of communication and teaching, and not one of invention and discovery. Descartes had already realised 'in respect to Logic that the syllogisms and the greater part of the other teaching served better in explaining to others those things that one knows . . . than in learning what is new' [(1)1.91; also 32]. And Webster says that 'It is cleer, that *Syllogizing*, and *Logical* invention are but a resumption of that which was known before, and that which we know not, *Logick* cannot find out' [38]. Such criticism is perhaps less than fair to Aristotle. One of his commentators suggests that 'the theory of demonstrative science was never meant to guide or formalise research: it is concerned exclusively with the teaching of facts already won'.[4] It carries more weight against his seventeenth-century followers. Though Sergeant's writings do not question its 'communicative function' they 'call attention primarily to the investigative function of Peripatetic logic' [*Howell* 70].

Sergeant thought the theory of *scientia* was most clearly applicable to mathematics. This is not surprising in view of the likelihood that the theory took mathematics as its model from the outset. Aristotle's examples indicate he initially had in mind the sciences of arithmetic and geometry. Indeed he points out that the word 'axiom' is borrowed from them [*Metaphysics* 1005a20]. For his part, Locke allows that the theory might plausibly *seem* applicable to mathematics [IV.xii.2]. But he is certain that really it is not:

> If any one will consider, he will (I guess) find, that the great advancement and certainty of real Knowledge, which Men arrived to in these Sciences, was not owing to the influence of these Principles, nor derived from any peculiar advantage they received from two or three general Maxims laid down in the beginning. [IV.xii.3]

What then is Locke's own view about how progress is made in mathematics? How indeed, if the Scholastic account of it is completely wrong, is our knowledge in any field to be extended and developed? He says at this point that the way men in fact made mathematical 'advancement' was 'from the clear, distinct, complete Ideas their Thoughts were employ'd about, and the relation of Equality and Excess so clear between some of them, that they had an intuitive Knowledge . . . and this without the help of those Maxims' [IV.xii.3]. But this does little more than simply say what knowledge is. We already know it consists in intuitively perceiving the connexion between ideas. It doesn't explain how we can advance and get more of it. We have seen in this section how Locke thinks we can't do it. We can now return to where we left matters at the end of the last section and see how he thinks we can.

Notes

[1] D.A.Givner, 'Scientific preconceptions in Locke's philosophy of language', *Journal of the History of Ideas*, 23 (1962), p. 352.

[2] Such books will explain Locke's technical references in IV.xvii. 4-8 to 'mode', 'figure', '*medius terminus*', 'extremes', 'major', 'minor', 'general', 'particular', 'form', 'rules of syllogism'.

[3] Locke sometimes makes allusions to the technicalities of disputation. He refers, for example, to 'topics', 'distinguishing', 'questioner', 'answerer', 'resolving' [(5) 3.223, 262-3, 9.178, III.x.12, IV.xvii.5].

[4] J. Barnes, 'Aristotle's Theory of Demonstration', *Articles on Aristotle*, vol. 1, ed. J. Barnes, M. Schofield, R. Sorabji (Duckworth, London, 1975), p.77; also 85.

9 The Extent and Improvement of Knowledge

If the Scholastic account is unsatisfactory how should we set about making intellectual discoveries and extending our knowledge? Book IV, chapter xii, 'On the Improvement of Knowledge', begins an answer. The question is closely connected with the one Locke set himself at the beginning of the *Essay* about whether there are any limits to the possible extent of knowledge. For whatever it is we should do to acquire new knowledge the further question will arise whether our procedure will always be successful. Book IV, chapter iii, 'The Extent of Human Knowledge', begins an answer to this further question. The present section explains Locke's answer to these two questions about the extent and improvement of knowledge.

Knowledge is the perception of connexions between ideas. We know from section 7 that we can perceive these connexions, and so have knowledge, in geometry. Indeed this is so obvious that, as Locke says, 'It has been generally taken for granted, that Mathematicks alone are capable of demonstrative certainty' [IV.ii.9]. We noted in section 7, however, that he does not go along with this. He thinks, for example, that it might be possible to 'place morality among the sciences capable of demonstration'. So there are things which lie beyond our present knowledge but to which, given a method, it might be extended. These are things within the reach of our *capacity* for knowledge. They are merely things to which *as a matter of fact* our knowledge does not extend. Are there things of which we not merely *do not*, but *could not* have knowledge? There are. Again as we noted in section 7, Locke recognises that sometimes we just cannot get knowledge. This is because of 'a want of a discoverable Connection between those Ideas which we have'

[IV.iii.28]. There are, that is to say, areas where all we can have is 'Faith, or Opinion' [IV.ii.14] and not 'universal or certain knowledge'.

To understand Locke's views on how knowledge is to be improved and extended and on the limits there are to this extension we need to know two things. We need to know why morality, though something about which we *do not* have knowledge, is nevertheless something about which we *could* have knowledge. What places this factual restriction on our knowledge, and how could we remove it? What should we do with our moral ideas to make them productive of knowledge and certainty? We need also to know why there are some fixed and irremovable boundaries to knowledge. Why is there sometimes 'a want of a discoverable Connection between those Ideas which we have'? Is there any explanation why some ideas have 'discoverable Connections' between them and others do not? Are they, perhaps, ideas of different sorts?

We will lack knowledge where we lack ideas, of course. 'There are some Things, and those not a few, that we are ignorant of for want of Ideas' [IV.iii.23]. Some things, such as the extremities of the universe, are too remote to be experienced. Others, such as the corpuscles of matter, are too minute [IV.iii.24-5]. Glanvill too partially explained our ignorance by limited experience and a consequent lack of ideas. 'Our *Senses* are very *scant* and *limited*; and the *Operations* of Nature *subtil*, and *various*' [(1) 17]. It is not that we are incapable of having ideas of, for example, size and shape. It is just that, our eyes not being telescopic or microscopic, we cannot learn about the size and shape of the very remote or of the very minute. But there is another more serious limit on the ideas we may have. Normally-sighted people have ideas of more sorts, ideas of colours for example, than do the blind who lack a dimension of sense. So perhaps 'Creatures in other parts of the Universe . . . by the Assistance of Senses and Faculties more or perfecter, than we have, or different from ours' have more ideas than we have [IV.iii.23].

Having ideas is merely a necessary not a sufficient condition for knowledge. In order to perceive immediate connexions between ideas we must also think clearly. We must 'fix in our

Minds clear, distinct and complete Ideas, as far as they are to be had, and annex to them proper and constant Names' [IV.xii.6]. But even when we have clear ideas in our minds and have intuitive knowledge by their means, we may still lack demonstrative knowledge that is open to us. We may not order our thoughts properly and stay in ignorance 'for want of finding out those intermediate Ideas' [IV.iii.30].

So it is often possible to extend and develop our knowledge. But we don't do it by deriving new conclusions from a basis of maxims, first principles, and definitions. We do it by avoiding ambiguous words, keeping our ideas clear, and by looking carefully for connexions between them. Given the ideas we have, and given clear, careful, and methodical thought, we can go far. Given care we might 'from very plain and easy beginnings, by gentle degrees, and a continued Chain of Reasonings, proceed to the discovery and demonstration of Truths, that appear at first sight beyond humane Capacity' [IV.xii.7].

But are there any limits to what can be done in this way? Are there any truths which in reality, not merely at first sight, lie 'beyond humane Capacity'? Locke thinks there are. '[A]nother cause of Ignorance . . . is a want of a discoverable Connection between those Ideas which we have' [IV.iii.28]. Knowledge consists in the perception of connexion between ideas and can extend no further than that. There are cases where, even given clear, careful and methodical thought, we can perceive no connexions between our ideas.

With some of our ideas 'there are certain Relations, Habitudes, and Connexions, so visibly included in the Nature of the Ideas themselves, that we cannot conceive them separable from them'. Here 'we are capable of certain and universal Knowledge' [IV.iii.29]. For example, 'the Idea of a right-lined Triangle necessarily carries with it an equality of its Angles to two right ones' [IV.iii.29]. Having followed a demonstration of this we can perceive that it is so. But in other cases, try as we might, we can see no such connexions. Here 'we are utterly uncapable of universal and certain Knowledge' [IV.iii.28].

Locke cites various cases like this in IV.iii.28-9. We know that pain can be produced by a sharp object coming into contact with our bodies. But there is 'no conceivable connexion

between any impulse of any sort of Body, and any perception
. . . which we find in our Minds'. We know also that, at will, we
can move our bodies. But how 'thought should produce a
motion' is equally remote 'from the nature of our Ideas'. We will
consider these cases in detail in section 17. A third and very
important case where 'we can have no universal certainty',
where 'we are not capable of a philosophical Knowledge'
[IV.iii.29], concerns the qualities, powers, and operations of
things in the world. It appears, for example, that gold dissolves
in sulphuric acid. But we can discern no necessary connexion
between being gold and dissolving in sulphuric acid.

Cases of this third sort will concern us at length. In them
'Connexions and Dependancies being not discoverable in our
Ideas' [IV.iii.29] we are 'left only to Observation and Experiment' [IV.iii.28]. In learning about the properties of gold 'we
can go no farther than particular Experience informs us'
[IV.iii.29]. But observation and experiment can provide us only
with 'opinion'. Strictly speaking we can have no *knowledge* of the
properties of gold and other material things in the world. 'As to
a perfect *Science* of natural bodies', says Locke, 'we are . . . so far
from being capable of any such thing, that I conclude it lost
labour to seek after it' [IV.iii.29].

We shall consider in a while how Locke's distinction between
'knowledge' and 'opinion' is related to the older Aristotelian
distinction made in the same terms. For the moment we may
note that it has in effect been acknowledged by later philosophers. They too have distinguished cases where we can proceed
by 'the contemplation of our own abstract ideas', from cases
where there are no connexions visible between our ideas, where
we have to fall back onto observation and experiment. But later
philosophers have not always spoken of this as a distinction
between knowledge and something else. Instead they have
often spoken of two sorts of knowledge. What Locke calls 'knowledge' they have called *a priori*, non-empirical or conceptual
knowledge. What he calls 'opinion', they have called *a posteriori*,
empirical or experimental knowledge.

It is clear that Locke is right to say that knowledge acquired
by perceiving connexions amongst our ideas is 'certain and
universal'. When we see a connexion between being a triangle

and having angles equal to two right-angles we see that *all* triangles *must* have angles like that. We cannot, as Locke says, conceive the connexions as separable from the ideas [IV.iii.29]. On the other hand, when we can see no connexion between gold and dissolving in sulphuric acid, when we have learnt of this property of gold only from experience, we see only that gold does dissolve in sulphuric acid, not that it *must* do so. 'The Things that, as far as our Observation reaches, we constantly find to proceed regularly, we may conclude, do act by a Law set them; but yet by a Law, that we know not' [IV.iii.29]. We may suppose that it is universally and certainly true that gold dissolves in sulphuric acid. But relying as we have to on observation we cannot *know* that it is.

Locke's suggestions about the relevance of experiment and observation for finding out about the properties and powers of things in the world are part of the whole anti-Scholastic movement discussed in section 4. Bacon and his intellectual heirs in the Royal Society believed that the 'sciences, arts, and all human knowledge' had, in the hands of the Scholastics, come to a dead-end. They believed that the intellectual constructions of the past needed to be swept away and that a 'proper foundation' should be laid. Section 4 briefly mentioned that what they specifically had in mind for this 'foundation' was a mass of information about the natural world derived from careful pains-taking observation and methodical experiment. This brief mention needs filling out now as a background for Locke's references to observation and experiment.

Bacon recognised that people had earlier gone in for some collecting of the results of observation and experiment. But they had not done so in any systematic way. The 'foundation to build philosophy on' which *he* envisaged was hardly piecemeal and limited. It was to be literally universal. It would 'embrace . . . the Phenomena of the Universe; that is to say, experience of every kind' [4.8]. He stresses that 'special care is to be taken that it be of wide range and made to the measure of the universe. . . . For that fashion of taking few things into account, and pro-nouncing with reference to a few things, has been the ruin of everything' [4.255-6]. Bacon calls such a collection of facts a 'Natural and Experimental History' [4.251]. In a 'Catalogue of

Particular Histories' [4.265] he gives a list of 130 particular areas of suitable investigation, some of which he undertook himself. Its range is breathtaking, from a 'History of the Heavenly Bodies; or Astronomical History' through a 'History of Conception, Vivifaction, Gestation in the Womb, Birth, etc.' to a 'History of Glass and all vitreous substances, and of Glass-making'.

When Bacon speaks of a 'history', of the heavenly bodies for example, he does not mean an account of significant events in the *temporal* development of the universe. He means a methodical record, with no particular temporal reference, of natural phenomena and of the properties and powers of things. The idea of a 'history' in this sense was very common in the seventeenth century. Perhaps it survives today only in the phrase 'natural history', the name of the study of plants and animals.

The seventy-eighth item in Bacon's catalogue of particular histories is 'History of the Intellectual Faculties; Reflexion, Imagination, Discourse, Memory, etc.'. It has been suggested that Locke's *Essay* is, though wider in scope, in effect just such a history.[1] Locke does indeed describe himself as having 'given . . . a short, and, I think, a true history of the rise and original of human knowledge . . . wherein I must appeal to your experience and observation whether I am in the right: the best way to come to truth being to examine things as really as they are' [(2) 83].

Bacon's idea that systematic observation and experiment is needed as the foundation for a satisfactory 'natural philosophy' did not go unchallenged. Sergeant was sure 'the Way of *Experiments*' was a complete waste of time. 'This Method, *alone*, and Unassisted by *Principles*, is utterly Incompetent or Unable to beget *Science*' [(1) preface]. Yet it was endorsed by many others. Webster said that 'It cannot be expected that *Physical* science will arrive at any wished perfection, unless the ways and means, so judiciously laid down by our learned Countreyman the Lord *Bacon*, be observed'. He urged that the results of 'diligent observation' and 'luciferous experiments' need to be 'recorded in a general history of natural things, that so every age and generation, proceeding in the same way, and upon the same principles, may dayly go on with the work, to the building up of a well-grounded and lasting Fabrick, which indeed is the only true way for the instauration and advance of learning and knowledge' [105]. Power agreed that 'These are the days that must lay a new Foundation of a more magnificent Philosophy, never to be overthrown: that will Empirically and Sensibly canvass the *Phaenomena* of Nature . . . . [T]his is the way, and no other, to build a true and permanent Philosophy' [192]. Hooke also saw the need for a 'vast treasury of a philosophical history' [28] and hoped to play a modest part in its production. 'I have obtained my end, if my small labours shall be thought fit to take up some place in the large stock of natural observations, which so many hands are busy in providing' [5-6]. Finally, and as we might expect, Sprat's *History of the Royal Society* repeated the idea that 'The True Philosophy must be first of all begun, on a scrupulous, and severe examination of particulars' [31; also 111, 115 f., 331, 327, 336 f.].

It was mentioned earlier in this section that Locke's distinction between 'knowledge' and 'opinion' looks forward to a more recent distinction between *a priori* and *a posteriori* knowledge. Does it also look back to Aristotle's distinction between 'scientific knowledge' and 'opinion'? It certainly alludes to Aristotle's and takes over its terminology. Aristotle's distinction was a commonplace in the seventeenth century. It was repeated by Spencer [157] and Sergeant [(1) 322], for example. But the precise details of the relation between the knowledge/opinion distinction of the Scholastic tradition and what Locke, antagonist of that tradition, makes of it are not straightforward.

It is easy to make some initial comparisons. As Aristotle defines and explains it, knowledge has to do with necessities, with what must be so and cannot be otherwise. For Locke, too, knowledge is universal and certain. But whereas Aristotle thinks that knowledge has a structure and it is to be acquired only on the basis of a demonstrative syllogism which has maxims and definitions for premises, Locke does not. As we know, he places no particular value on syllogistic methods or on general abstract maxims.

The relation between Aristotle's and Locke's 'opinion' is more complicated. According to the traditional view of 'opinion' it has to do with contingencies, with things which might have been otherwise. It may seem at first sight that this is equally so for Locke. But there is a certain complexity in his position. On the one hand he certainly does not think that we *know* that gold dissolves in sulphuric acid. We have knowledge only when we perceive a necessary connexion between our ideas, and there is no necessary connexion visible between our idea of gold and the idea of dissolving in sulphuric acid. For us there can be no 'universal certainty' about this property of gold. On the basis of observation and experience, which is all we have to go on, all we can tell is that gold does so dissolve, not that it must. On the other hand, however, the fact that *for us* there is no 'universal certainty' about this property of gold need not mean that there is no such certainty in fact. If *we* have no knowledge here it need not be because there are no necessary connexions of the sort which form the basis for knowledge. The fact that there is no necessary connexion *visible* need not mean that there is not one there. So while for the Scholastic tradition 'opinion' concerns contingencies, for Locke it concerns what to us *seem like* contingencies, but what in reality may be universal certainties. This subtlety in Locke's position will be studied later. For the moment we should turn to another but connected point of comparison between Locke and the Scholastic tradition.

We have seen that one feature of that tradition was the idea that the pursuit of *scientia* is the proper use of man's reason. Mere opinion is not worth serious and systematic attention. Indeed, the very use of the word 'system' is out of place in connexion with 'opinion'. It is clear, however, that Locke thinks that 'opinion' *is* well worth having and searching after. He thinks that observation of and experiment on things in the world in order to discover their properties, is a worthwhile activity. In effect he thinks that there can be a system or body of 'opinion'. The system of 'opinion' he has in mind he calls 'natural philosophy'. This, of course, is 'not capable of being made a science'. After all it is based on observation and experiment and not on the perception of connexion between ideas – though he does occasionally speak of 'experimental knowledge' instead of 'opinion' [IV.iii.29, vi.7]. To this extent Locke agrees with his Scholastic opponent Sergeant that 'the Way of *Experiments* cannot be a True METHOD TO SCIENCE' [(1)

preface]. But even if properly speaking not a science, it is still worth systematic pursuit and investigation.

The last paragraph deals only with Locke. This was because *his* term 'opinion' was being discussed. But of course the idea of a systematic and serious observationally and experimentally based study of nature called 'natural philosophy' was one Locke shared with others. Indeed section 4 noted that natural science as we have it today is a direct descendent of the 'natural philosophy' of the seventeenth century. As we have seen many times before, over and over in that century people complained that there are areas and methods of serious investigation which are just not approachable and accounted for by Scholastic doctrines. 'This *School Philosophy* is altogether void of true and infallible demonstration, observation, and experiment, the only certain means, and instruments to discover, and anatomize natures occult and central operations; which are found out by laborious tryals, manual operations, assiduous observations, and the like' [*Webster* 68].

So one very important limit on our knowledge is the whole area of what was known as 'natural philosophy'. We cannot have knowledge of the properties and powers of, for example, gold, because there are no necessary connexions visible between the relevant ideas. Unlike the study of the properties of triangles, the study of gold's properties is by way of observation and experiment. Now that we have reached this conclusion it is worthwhile repeating some questions which were asked at the beginning of this section. Why is there this boundary to our knowledge? Why is there, in these cases, 'a want of a discover-able Connection between those Ideas which we have'? Is there any explanation why some idea have 'discoverable connections' between them and others do not? Are they ideas of different sorts perhaps?

The *Essay* contains answers to these questions. To find them it is useful to contrast 'natural philosophy' with ethics. 'Natural philosophy' is an area into which our knowledge does not extend. Ethics is another such area. But according to Locke though we do not have knowledge in ethics we *could* have. What is it about our ethical ideas that makes this possible? The brief answer is that our ethical ideas are what Locke calls *real essences*.

At IV.xii.7 he asks whether the mathematical method can be further extended. He says that it can be, into areas where we know *real essences*. It cannot into areas where we don't. 'If other Ideas, that are the real, as well as nominal Essences of their Species, were pursued in the way familiar to Mathematicians, they would carry our Thoughts farther'. But, he continues, 'In our search after the Knowledge of Substances . . . [w]e advance not here, as in the other (where our abstract Ideas are real as well as nominal Essences' [IV.xii.9].

It seems then that there are no necessary connexions visible between our ideas in natural philosophy because our ideas there concern *substances* whose real essences we do not know. Whereas there are necessary connexions visible between our ideas in mathematics because we are concerned there with *modes* whose real essences we do know. Clearly our next task must be to understand this distinction between modes and substances.

Notes

1 N.Wood, 'The Baconian Character of Locke's *Essay*', *Studies in History and Philosophy of Science*, 6 (1975), p.63.

CHAPTER III

10 Complex Ideas: Relations

We noted in section 6 that much of Book II, 'Of Ideas', discusses various sorts of complex idea. II.xii.3 distinguishes three sorts: *modes*, *substances*, and *relations*. Modes, such as 'triangle', 'gratitude', 'murder', are said to 'contain not in them the supposition of subsisting by themselves, but are considered as Dependences on, or Affections of Substances' [II.xii.4]. Substances, such as 'lead', 'man', 'sheep', are 'distinct particular things subsisting by themselves' [II.xii.6]. Finally, '[t]he last sort of complex Ideas, is that we call *Relation*, which consists in the consideration and comparing one Idea with another' [II.xii.7].

When they are first mentioned, modes, substances, and relations alike are not things about or of which we may have ideas. They are ideas themselves. Locke continues to speak of modes (and relations) in this way. 'Ideas of modes' simply are 'ideas that are modes'. But substances are treated as things rather than ideas, so that 'ideas of substances' are 'ideas of things which are substances'. What lies behind this difference is that the distinction between an idea and what the idea is of is not sharp in the case of modes (and relations) but is in the case of substances. In the following sections it will sometimes be useful to distinguish between 'substance-ideas' and 'substances'.

Relations are the least important of the three sorts of complex idea. They play a relatively small part in the *Essay*. In the end Locke often treats them along with modes. We need not spend much time on them.

A certain addition to the fourth edition of the *Essay* is often taken as showing that relations are no longer being considered as complex ideas. In this passage (in II.xii.1) Locke distinguishes three different acts or operations of the mind which we may perform on simple ideas. The first of these, 'combining', is that by which 'all Complex Ideas are made'. This might give the impression that the results of the other two, 'Ideas of Relations' (got by 'setting . . . [two ideas] by one another, so as to take a view of them at once, without uniting them into one') and 'General Ideas' (made by 'Abstraction') should not count as complex ideas. The fact is, however, that this fourth edition addition is not a reclassification of ideas. It does not mean that there are ideas which are neither simple nor complex but of some third sort. It is rather that Locke's interest here is in the *different ways* in which complex ideas are formed. So, since modes and substances are formed in a way different from relations, he uses 'complex ideas' in a restricted sense to refer solely to them and not to all complex ideas as such.[1]

Even though Locke does not change his mind about relations being complex ideas it might still be said that he should have done. For the connexion between simple ideas and relations is rather different from that between simple ideas and other sorts of complex idea. Officially Locke would deny this. 'All the Ideas we have of Relation', he says, 'are made up, as the others are, only of simple Ideas' [II.xxv.11]. But as his commentators have noted, relations do not resolve into simple ideas in the same way that modes and substance-ideas do [*Gibson* 67; *O'Connor* 58]. These last two sorts of complex idea are 'made up of' simple ideas in relatively straightforward way. They are composed out of them and can be analysed into them. But it will be clear from Locke's account of relations that it cannot be in this way that they 'all terminate in, and are concerned about . . . simple Ideas' [II.xxv.9]. What account of relations does Locke give?

'The nature . . . of Relation', he says, 'consists in the refer-ring, or comparing two things, one to another; from which comparison, one or both comes to be denominated' [II.xxv.5]. Now some words or phrases, such as 'bigger than' or 'whiter', are quite clearly relational. Their superficial grammar requires two things. It makes no sense simply to say 'John is bigger than'. But, as can be seen from the example 'Caius is a father' [II.xxv.5], a term is counted as relative not simply when mere grammar requires more than one thing. A term is relative also when our thought is 'led to something beyond' the one thing mentioned [II.xxv.1].

One feature of relative terms, therefore, is that there are two things compared or related or, when only one thing is mentioned, the mind is 'led' from one thing to another. A second is that the two things are compared *in some respect* or other, or are related *by reference to* something. There has to be an 'occasion, why the Mind thus brings two things together, and, as it were, takes a view of them at once, though still considered as distinct' [II.xxv.1]. Caius is related to Sempronia by being her husband. What Locke calls the 'occasion' or 'foundation' of the relation is the 'Contract, and Ceremony of Marriage with Sempronia' [II.xxv.1]. Caius is related to his son by being his father. Here the occasion or foundation lies in the 'Circumstances of . . . origin or beginning' of the boy, i.e. in biological facts about his birth [II.xxviii.2].

This analysis of relations did not originate with Locke. It represents something he *accepted* from the Scholastics. They recognised three elements in a relation. With fatherhood, the father is the *subject, in which* the relation is; the son is the *term, towards which* the relation is directed; and the act of generation is the *foundation, by which* the relation is constituted.[2] These three elements are clearly there in the account given of relations in Burgersdijck's famous scholastic *Logic*. Besides the subject ('to which the Relation is attributed'), the term ('to which the Subject is referred') relations 'require a Foundation . . . by whose Means the Relation accrews to the Subject' or 'upon which this Relation is founded'. A servant is 'the Servant of one; because by him he has been either *saved* or *purchased*, etc.' [1.21-2].

Given this account of relations, what does Locke mean when he says that relations 'terminate in' simple ideas? On one view he means 'the related terms *are* simple ideas' or 'the related terms are complex ideas which themselves "terminate in" simple ideas' [*O'Connor* 59; *Perry* 222]. According to this, when one colour is *brighter* than another the relation 'terminates in' the simple ideas of the colours. Similarly, given that Caius is a husband, his relation to Sempronia terminates in the complex ideas of Caius and Sempronia, complex ideas which are themselves composed out of simple ideas. In effect this says that what Locke means by the 'termination' of a relation is the two things related, the 'subject' and the 'term' of the Scholastics. But this is simply wrong. By the 'termination' of a relation Locke means what both he and the Scholastics call its 'occasion' or 'foundation'. What Caius' being a husband terminates in, is founded in, is not him and Sempronia. It terminates in 'the Contract, and Ceremony of Marriage' which brought it about that they were married [II.xxv.1]. That relations do not 'terminate' in their terms but in their 'foundations' or 'occasions' is clear from at least two passages [II.xxv.8, xxviii.18]. It is clear also from Locke's promise (at the end of II.xxv) to give illustrations of the 'termination' of relations in simple ideas. For when he comes to give them (at the beginning of II.xxviii) they are described as 'occasions . . . of comparing, or referring'.

Locke's remarks that relations are not 'contained in the real existence of Things, but [are] something extraneous and superinduced' [II.xxv.8] is worth noting because of the amount of discussion it has provoked. Gibson exaggerates when he says that 'Locke's denial of the reality of relations is too prominent to be overlooked' [193]. But his explanation of what Locke means seems right. Relations are extraneous and superinduced because some relative terms can cease to apply to an object without there being any change in that thing. Caius ceases to be a father when his *son dies* [II.xxv.5]. One door ceases to be the same colour as another when the *other* door *is painted*.

Unlike relations, the other two sorts of complex idea, modes and substances, are extremely important for Locke's account of the original, certainty and extent of knowledge. We shall need to spend some considerable time on them. What Locke says needs to be seen against a background of discussion about 'substance' which goes back at least to Aristotle. This will be the first topic of the next section.

Notes

[1] See D.J. Rabb, 'Are Locke's Ideas of Relations Complex?', *The Locke Newsletter*, 5 (1974).

[2] See R.P. Phillips, *Modern Thomistic Philosophy*, vol. 1 (Burns, Oates and Co., London, 1934), vol. 1, p.80.

11 Substances: Real and Nominal Essences

Aristotle's views on 'substance' are mainly in his *Categories* and *Metaphysics*. The *Categories* lists ten 'kinds of predicate'. Roughly speaking, a predicate in the category of *substance*, the first of the ten, tells us what some individual thing *is*. For example we may be told that Socrates is a man. Socrates, this man, is a substance. Predicates in the other nine categories tell us what substances *are like* in respect of *quantity* (e.g. three feet long), *quality* (e.g. white), *place* (e.g. in Greece), and so on. Aristotle further distinguishes between *first substance* and *second substance*. First substances are individual things such as the particular man Socrates. Second substances are the species or genera to which first substances belong. 'For instance, the individual man is included in the species "man", and the genus to which the species belongs is "animal"; these, therefore – that is to say, the species "man" and the genus "animal" – are termed secondary substances' [2a16-18].

Aristotle's followers later called all the nine non-substantial predicates 'accidents'. Thus Thomas Aquinas (1225-74) speaks in his *Summa Theologiae* of 'nine categories of accidental being' [1a.28,2]. This meant that there was a single contrast between *substance* and *accident*. We have already encountered 'accident' as a technical term in Aristotelian philosophy in section 8. A distinction was made there between *separable* and *inseparable accidents* (or properties). 'Accidents' as they appear in the doctrine of the *Categories* came to be called predicamental accidents. 'Accidents' understood as the separable accidents of the theory of real definitions were called predicable accidents. Something is an accident in the first of these senses just so long as it is not a substance. Whether it is an accident in the second sense depends entirely on what kind of thing it is an attribute of.

What is a separable accident of one kind of thing may not be of another.

The relation between first substances, or individual things, and accidents is that substances underlie or have accidents predicated of them. In a typical passage Aristotle says that 'primary substances are most properly so called, because they underlie and are the subjects of everything else' [2b38]. They are called substances 'because they are not predicated of a subject but everything else is predicated of them' [*Metaphysics* 1017b13-14]. He also says that substances are what 'can be without other things, while the others cannot be without *them*' [1019a4].

They are, that is to say, 'self-subsistent' [1031a28]. As Aquinas puts it, 'to exist separately and to be a particular thing seem to belong chiefly to substance'.[1] Statements like this set the scene for post-Aristotelian discussions of substances, both before and after Aquinas. Passages which echo, or explicitly refer to Aristotle are common in seventeenth-century texts. Spencer says that 'A singular thing, is most properly, a substance; because, all other things, be attributed thereunto, and that, attributed unto none' [16]. Burgersdijck says that 'A Substance is a Being subsisting of it self, and subject to Accidents' [1.8]. Pierre Du Moulin (1568-1658) says in his *Elements of Logick* (1624) that 'A substance is that which subsisteth by itselfe . . . . An Accident is that which cannot subsist of itselfe, but must have a subject or substance to uphold it' [4].

Locke's initial definitions of substances and modes should be read against this background. When he first makes it, the distinction between the two sorts of idea is closely related to the traditional distinction between substance and accident. He describes substances as 'such combinations of simple Ideas, as are taken to represent distinct particular things subsisting by themselves; in which the supposed, or confused Idea of Substance, such as it is, is always the first and chief' [II.xii.6]. As defined here substance-ideas are, in effect, simply ideas of Aristotelian first substances, ideas of particular things.

The ideas on the other side of Locke's distinction, modes, are 'complex Ideas, which however compounded, contain not in them the supposition of subsisting by themselves, but are con-

sidered as Dependences on, or Affections of Substances; such as
the Ideas signified by the Words *Triangle, Gratitude, Murther*,
etc.' [II.xii.4]. They are not, however, straightforwardly identical with the accidents of the traditional theory. In his replies to
Stillingfleet Locke does write as though they are [(5) 4.19]. But
he uses the word 'accident' at other places in the *Essay* and
elsewhere explicitly mentions the traditional substance/
accident distinction. This makes it significant that he does not
do so here at II.xii.4 when he is defining modes [II.xiii. 17,19,
xxiii.2, 15]. Furthermore, if we suppose that the interchange-
able use of 'mode' and 'accident' (as in the correspondence with
Stillingfleet) is standard, we should note that here in the *Essay*
Locke apologises for using 'the word *Mode*, in somewhat a
different sence from its ordinary signification' [II.xii.4]. One
commentator who relates Locke's substance/mode distinction
to the 'commonsense distinction between things and their properties' says that it is 'a variation' of it [*O'Connor* 52]. And it is
indeed clear that 'the Ideas signified by the Words *Triangle,
Gratitude, Murther'* are not accidents. Nevertheless it is not too
difficult to begin to see how, like accidents, they are 'Dependences on, or Affections of Substances' like lead or man. For
there to be gratitude and murder there need to be grateful men
and their acts, murderers and their victims. Similarly the triangles we meet with in the world need to be made from lead or
some other material.

But we need not puzzle too much about the precise relation
between Locke's first definition of substances and modes and
the traditional substance/accident distinction. It is plain from
the later and far more important discussions of substances and
modes that substance-ideas are, in the end, not to be understood as ideas of Aristotelian first substances. They are, in the
end, more like ideas of Aristotelian second substances, kinds of
thing. It is also plain that to understand the notion of a mode
there is little point in trying to develop a full account of how
exactly gratitude and murder are 'dependent on' substances.
The idea of 'dependence' in no way forms the focus of interest in
Locke's later discussions of modes and substances. These begin
in Book II with chapters specifically devoted to each sort of idea
[xxii, xxiii]. It is better, however, to look first at Book III. For

here is the first explicit mention of a distinction which is
crucially important for understanding Locke's notions of modes
and substances. This is the distinction, to which we should now
turn our attention, between *real* and *nominal essences*. Until section 14 it will concern us only as it applies to substances.

In Book III, then, substance-ideas are ideas of *kinds* of thing.
They relate more closely to Aristotelian second substances than
to his individual first substances. From III.vi.1-2 we learn that
'Names of Substances' are the common nouns for kinds of
naturally occurring things such as men and horses, or of
materials such as lead or gold. Of these 'Sorts, or Species' of
thing Locke says this:

> The measure and boundary of each Sort, or Species, whereby it is con-
> stituted that particular Sort, and distinguished from others, is that we call
> its Essence, which is nothing but that abstract Idea to which the Name is
> annexed: So that every thing contained in that Idea, is essential to that
> Sort. This, though it be all the Essence of natural Substances, that we
> know, or by which we distinguish them into Sorts; yet I call it by a peculiar
> name, the *nominal Essence*, to distinguish it from that real Constitution of
> Substances, upon which depends this *nominal Essence*, and all the Properties
> of that Sort; which therefore, as has been said, may be called the *real*
> *Essence*.

He then explains this distinction between real and nominal
essence. The nominal essence of gold is 'that complex Idea the
word *Gold* stands for, let it be, for instance, a Body yellow, of a
certain weight, malleable, fusible, and fixed'. The real essence,
on the other hand, is 'the constitution of the insensible parts of
that Body, on which those Qualities, and all the other Properties of Gold depend'. To understand this it is useful to consider Locke's analogical application of the notions of real and
nominal essence to the Strasbourg cathedral clock.

Over the years there have been three clocks at Strasbourg
cathedral. The one Locke knew was the second of them, built in
the sixteenth century and surviving into the nineteenth. There
is a five-foot high model of it in the British Museum. Locke
refers to it twice by name. It is clear from what he says and from
the fact that others such as Boyle refer to 'the famous clock at
Strasburgh' [2.7] that it was regarded with some awe and
wonder. It is easy to see why. At the base of the clock there was a

celestial globe with revolving sun and moon, surrounded by a calendar which indicated the day. Above this there appeared, each at their respective time, the gods that give their names to the days of the week. Then, still higher up the fifty-five foot construction, pointers indicated the time of day and figures of genii moved on the hour. Next was an astrolabe showing the varying positions of the planets. There then came four statues, representing the four periods of life, which struck the quarter-hours on cymbals. A bell for marking the hours was sounded by a figure of Death, who moved in dumb show with a representation of Christ. Finally, on a side turret, was a mechanical cock, designed with opening beak and flapping wings to crow daily at noon. This was struck by lightning when Locke was eight, and thereafter was made to work only on Sundays and feast days.

The Strasbourg cathedral clock was obviously unique. It was, as the phrase has it, the only one of its kind. But even without imagining more of its kind ever being built we can think or speak of *the kind of clock* of which the one in Strasbourg was the only one. We could, that is to say, speak of 'Strasbourg-type clocks'. We could use these words as the name of, as Locke says, 'a sort, or species' of clock. They would parallel the words 'man' or 'horse' as the names of sorts or species of animal. The idea of a Strasbourg-type clock would be no more the idea of a particular individual clock, the clock in Strasbourg cathedral than the substance-idea of a horse is the idea of a particular individual horse, say Bucephalus.

Now to be of the Strasbourg-type a clock would need to have certain very definite characteristics. It would need to exhibit the behaviour of the Strasbourg clock as described above. It would need to have a figure of Death sounding a bell on the hour. It would need to show the positions of the planets. Besides all this, however, any such clock would also need to have a certain internal mechanism which would enable it to have these characteristics and behaviour. A clock with different internal construction could not be a Strasbourg-type clock for it would not be able to function outwardly as the Strasbourg clock did. This internal mechanism, the mechanism which would be required for a clock to perform in the requisite manner, is thought of by Locke as being, in effect, the *real essence* of a

Strasbourg-type clock. The real essence of a given type is whatever it is about things of that type which gives them the properties and characteristics of that type. It is that 'on which all the
properties of the Species depend, and from which alone they all
flow' [III.v.14].

On the other hand, the *nominal essence* of a Strasbourg-type
clock, is, roughly speaking, whatever would be said in answer to
the question 'What is a Strasbourg-type clock?'. It is clear, of
course, that different people will answer this question differently. If it were put to a man in the street, to (as Locke says)
'a gazing Country-man' who had been awestruck by the
appearance and performance of such a clock, the answer would
be in terms of the most noteworthy of its features. A clock of that
type, he might begin by saying, is a clock with a figure of
Death sounding the hours on a bell. Alternatively, however,
another man in the street, one who happened not to pass by on
the hour, might not make reference to the figure of Death. He
might have noticed the astrolabe showing the positions of the
planets. Now these passers-by have been struck by different
things. They think of Strasbourg-type clocks in different ways.
But they have in common that the significance such clocks have
for them lies in the clocks' observable characteristics and behaviour. They may both, therefore, be contrasted with an
horologist or some other person with an understanding of
clocks. For he, if asked what Strasbourg-type clocks are, would
not answer in terms of some or other of the observable characteristics. He would think rather in terms of the *real essence*, the
ingenious and complex mechanism which produces and
accounts for the observable behaviour which so impresses the
passers-by. It follows then that the *nominal essence* of a
Strasbourg-type clock varies from person to person. This has
the important consequences that in some cases (as in that of the
horologist) there is a coincidence between real essence and
nominal essence. In others there is no such coincidence. In
these cases the nominal essence has to do with the properties
and characteristics which the internal mechanism, the real
essence, gives rise to.

The distinction between the real and nominal essence of the
Strasbourg-type clock is not the same distinction as that

between an internal mechanism and the resultant publicly observable characteristics and behaviour. The real essence of that type of clock is whatever it is about clocks of that type which produces their characteristic behaviour. The nominal essence has to do with how that type of thing is identified and described. This may, as with a gazing countryman, involve the outward show. It may, as with the horologist, involve the inner mechanism. But different as they are, the two distinctions are closely connected. The first side of the one coincides with the first side of the other. The real essence of the clock just is its mechanism. It follows that if in a given case one could find no application for the distinction between characteristic observable features and what produces and accounts for them, then there would be no application for the notions of real and nominal essence. In particular, the notion of a real essence would have no place. These facts will turn out to be rather important. We will encounter cases where Locke does want to talk in terms of real and nominal essence, but where there appears to be no basis for a distinction between observable characteristics and what produces them.

We can easily apply these thoughts about real and nominal essence to substances such as lead, gold, horses. To begin with, just as there are typical features of the Strasbourg-type clock so there are easily observable and typical properties or qualities of gold. There are typical behaviour patterns of horses. Gold is yellow, malleable, fusible, soluble in some acids and not in others. Horses have a characteristic shape, eat grass and hay, and sometimes whinny and neigh. Now to think of gold or of horses as having a real essence will be to think that there is something about them which accounts for or gives rise to these outward characteristics and features. Locke does think just this. More specifically, he supposes that gold is constituted of minute atoms, 'insensible corpuscles' he calls them. These are of various sizes and move with various velocities. As he conceives it, the mechanical interaction of these corpuscles gives rise to gold's observed properties such as its yellow colour, and its solubility in certain acids. Observed changes in substances, such as the dissolving of gold in an acid, result from the changing motions and arrangements of the corpuscles of gold produced by the contact between them and those of the acid. The difference in qualities of different substances, such as the yellowness of gold and the silvery colour of lead, results from the differences in shape, size, arrangement and state of motion of their corpuscles. It is not so easy to see how the real essence of the horse could be interpreted along these corpuscular mechanical lines. We might, however, in terms rather too modern for Locke, understand it as its genetic makeup.

Just as the observable characteristics of a Strasbourg-type clock are associated with a certain internal mechanism of wheels and cogs, 'a real essence', so those of gold are associated with a certain arrangement of mechanically interacting corpuscles. But a difference between the two cases should be noted. It will be important later. The nominal essence of a Strasbourg-type clock might coincide with the real essence. It would for an horologist. But for all of us the nominal essence of gold and other substances has always to do with outer observable characteristics. Unlike God and the angels, we have no detailed knowledge or grasp of its real essence. So far as gold is concerned we are all 'gazing Country-men'.

Locke's understanding of the real essence of substances in terms of their corpuscular constitution is illustrated in many passages. He speaks of the properties of substances 'consisting in a Texture and Motion of Parts' [IV.iii.16], and of 'insensible Corpuscles, being the active parts of Matter, and the great Instruments of Nature' on which the qualities and operations of things depend [IV.iii.25; also II.xxiii.10.f.,III.vi.9, IV.iii.11, 13, 26]. The importance of this idea in Locke will occupy us in the next section.

Notes

[1] *Commentary on the Metaphysics of Aristotle*, trans. J.P. Rowan (Henry Regnery, Chicago, 1961), vol. 2, p.495.

12 Corpuscularian versus Scholastic Explanation

The scientifically sophisticated might find Locke's idea of a corpuscular constitution primitive and underdeveloped. But the *general* idea that gold's properties are produced in the way outlined at the end of the last section will sound very plausible to a twentieth-century ear. It would have sounded plausible to many of Locke's contemporaries too. He was by no means the originator of the corpuscular account of matter, and by the time the *Essay* was published it was a commonplace. It originated in Greece in the fifth and fourth centuries B.C., with the philosophers Leucippus, Democritus, and Epicurus. It was then taken up afresh and revitalised in the seventeenth century by Galileo, Gassendi, and Hobbes.[1] It had patrons in the Royal Society and is closely associated both with it and with the new experimentally and observationally based science. This close association is perhaps more accidental than necessary. Hooke refers to 'the mechanical, the experimental philosophy' [3] as though they were both one. But there is no particular connexion between a belief in the compilation of natural histories of the properties of things and a belief that these are to be explained in corpuscular or mechanical terms.

Perhaps Locke got his ideas on this from his friend Boyle. Certainly Boyle was the most persistent and thorough seventeenth-century advocate of 'the corpuscular hypothesis'. A good deal of his extensive writing is taken up in one way or another with explanation and defence of it. Boyle begins with the idea that there is 'one catholick or universal matter common to all bodies, . . . a substance extended, divisible, and impenetrable' [3.15]. This is divided into parts because it has within it varying degrees and direction of local motion. The 'division of matter is frequently made into insensible corpuscles or par-

ticles' each of which has 'its own magnitude, or rather size, and
its own figure or shape' [3.16]. When considered in relation to
each other these corpuscles have a posture and an order [3.22].
Furthermore, 'when many corpuscles do so convene together as
to compose any distinct body, as a stone or a metal, then from
their other accidents (or modes) and from these two last mentioned, there doth emerge a certain disposition or contrivance of
parts in the whole, which we may call the texture of it' [3.22].
Finally 'it is from the size, shape, and motion of the small parts
of matter and the texture that results from the manner of their
being disposed in any one body, that the colour, odour, taste
and other qualities of that body are to be derived' [3.31]. For
example, the properties of gold of being soluble in *aqua regia* and
not in *aqua fortis* 'are not in the gold any thing distinct from its
peculiar texture' [3.18]. Much of Boyle's work is devoted to
showing in detail how the results of various observations and
experiments are to be explained in these terms.[2]

The idea that the properties of material substances arise from
their corpuscular constitution was an orthodoxy when the *Essay*
was published. But it was a relatively new orthodoxy. The
conception of how the various properties and powers of things
are to be explained which corpuscularianism provides replaced
another conception. The real essence of a substance such as
gold is, for Locke, its inner corpuscular mechanical constitution. But this is merely his *interpretation of*, his way of giving
content to, the idea of a real essence. This is not what the phrase
'real essence' *means*. What the phrase means is, that 'on which
all the properties of the Species depend, and from which alone
they all flow' [III.v.14]. In the seventeenth century there was
another interpretation of the idea of there being something
about things of a certain kind which accounts for their characteristic properties, one which the corpuscular interpretation
began to supplant. It will be no surprise that this was one given
by the Scholastics of the time.

There were, then, two divergent ideas about the way explanation of the properties of things should proceed. As the *Essay*
puts it, 'Concerning the real Essences of corporeal Substances
. . . there are . . . two Opinions'. One supposes 'a certain
number of those Essences, according to which, all natural

things are made, and wherein they do exactly every one of them partake, and so become of this or that Species'. The other and 'more rational Opinion' supposes 'all natural Things to have a real, but unknown Constitution of their insensible Parts, from which flow those sensible Qualities, which serve us to distinguish them one from another, according as we have Occasion to rank them into sorts, under common Denominations' [III.iii.17].

The second of these two interpretations of the idea of a real essence, the one Locke finds the 'more rational', is simply the one we have already seen him advocating. It is the corpuscular account of Boyle and other Royal Society fellows. The first 'opinion', which Locke comments has 'very much perplexed the Knowledge of natural Things', is to be attributed to the Scholastics. Like so much else in Scholasticism it derives ultimately from Aristotle, though no doubt it underwent various mutations, notably at the hands of Aquinas. It has come to be known as the theory of hylemorphism. Aspects of it were touched on in section 8, in connexion with the Aristotelian theory of *scientia*. We there came across the idea of forms, natures, or essences, and the idea of their definition which should preface each science.

Each individual first substance is seen as being a composite of *form* (*morphe*) and *matter* (*hyle*). An amount of *material* like bronze can be made, or *formed*, into a statue or into a bowl. Similarly a man could be considered as flesh, bones and blood *informed* by humanity. But these materials are unformed matter only relative and prior to their being fashioned into or forming a statue or a man. They are not absolutely unformed or *primary matter* (*materia prima*). They are, after all, bronze, or flesh and bones. They should be thought of as *secondary matter* (*materia secunda*). This is itself a composite out of primary matter and a form such as that of bronze or of flesh.

Now it will be remembered from the beginning of the last section that there are two main categories or kinds of predicate, *substance* and *accident*. Corresponding to these there are two kinds of form, *substantial* and *accidental*. Just as some prime matter might take on the substantial form of bronze, so some bronze might take on the accidental form of being shaped in a certain way. An individual substance such as a man is a composite of matter and the substantial form of humanity. He might, however, have taken on also the accidental form of being educated. The elements of this analysis of first substances into matter and form were used and developed in various ways. They were, for example, used as the basis for an account of change. A 'composite' or 'concrete' whole of substantial form and matter was said to be what remained constant through accidental change. Examples of this would be bronze changing from one shape to another, or a man becoming educated. Similarly, prime matter was said to be what remained constant through substantial change, as when some wine turns into vinegar. But for the present purposes the most important role the analysis had was as part of the doctrine of the four causes. The roundness of a bowl or the shape of a statue were, we may remember from section 8, their formal causes. Thus a certain substantial form, for example that of gold, gives one sort of explanation, a 'formal' explanation, why the matter it is is of that kind. Similarly a certain accidental form, for example that of shape or fluidity was thought of as that which 'makes' some substance such as bronze of water have some accident or other and which explains, formally, why it is, for example, square or fluid.

According to the Aristotelian theory of *scientia* each science must begin with a definition of the nature or substantial form of the various species with which it deals. It must on the basis of the definitions and other first principles then demonstrate that the properties or inseparable accidents of the species in question must belong to it. This theory combines with hylemorphism to give a conception of how the various properties and qualities of things come about and how they are to be explained. Suppose it is asked why some gold has a certain attribute. Or suppose we want to know why a particular man has a certain feature. The answer depends in the first place on whether the attribute or feature is in the category of substance and hence has to do with substantial form and the relevant definition. For example gold is of the *genus* metal and it is a *differentia* of men that they are rational. So if the questions were why the gold is a metal or why the man is rational the answer would be that it is of the essence, nature, or form of gold to be a metal, and of men to be rational.

On the other hand the attribute or feature may have been in one of the accidental categories. In this case the answer why it is present turns on whether it is an inseparable accident, a genuine property, or is a separable accident. An example of the first of these would, in the case of man, be risibility, the capacity to laugh. This is not part of man's essence or form but it is related to it in that, as the Scholastics put it, it 'flows', 'derives', or 'emanates' from it. The general idea is that, as Aquinas says, 'a thing's characteristic operations derive from its substantial form' [*Summa Theologiae* 3a.75, 6]. Thus Burgersdijck explains that properties 'flow . . . *from the Essence of the Subject*; as *Risibility from the rational Soul*' [1.41]. Similarly Spencer says that since 'aptnes unto laughing' is an inseparable accident or property of men, since 'No man wants it, none but man hath it, and all men have it alwaies', it 'floweth . . . from' their form, 'as a natural emanation' [59-60]. In such cases the aim of a scientific demonstration would be the production of a syllogistic argument such that the derivation of the conclusion from the premisses mirrored the 'flowing' of the property from the form. As we have seen, the premisses of such a demonstration would give a definition of the relevant form or essence and the conclusion would state that things of the kind in question would have the property in question. The demonstration would explain, give us scientific knowledge of, how, for example, risibility follows or flows from the essence of man.

But besides inseparable accidents or properties there are also separable accidents. It is, for example, a separable accident of a man that he is educated, or of a piece of gold that it is in a fluid state. Here there can obviously be no question of why gold *as such*, or men *as such*, have the attribute. So there can be no question of how they relate to the substantial form. They are neither part of the relevant substantial forms nor do they flow from them. It is not of the nature or essence of man to be educated or of gold to be fluid. As Burgersdijck says, these 'properties flow from . . . *External Cause*' [1.41]. So far as formal explanation goes, all that can be said is that the man is educated because he embodies a certain accidental form, and that the gold is fluid because it has the accidental form of fluidity.

The hylemorphic conception of the production and explanation of the properties, powers, and behaviour of things obviously stands in contrast to that provided by corpuscularianism. According to hylemorphism what makes some unformed matter or *materia prima* to be gold is a certain substantial form. According to corpuscularianism, what makes Boyle's 'catholick or universal matter' to be gold is that its corpuscles are of a certain size and shape and are arranged in a certain way. According to hylemorphism the reason for some gold's having a certain characteristic would depend, as we have just seen, on how that characteristic relates to gold's essence or form. It may be part of the essence or nature of gold to have that characteristic, or the characteristic may be one which flows from gold's essence. Alternatively, however, the characteristic may, like the state it is in, be just an accidental feature of that piece of gold. In this case the reason would lie in the acquisition by the gold of a certain accidental form. On the other hand, the corpuscularian explanation of some gold's solubility in *aqua regia* or its being in a certain state would have to do with the arrangement of the corpuscles making it up. One way which has been suggested of making the contrast between hylemorphism and corpuscularianism is that the first appeals to form as an explanatory factor whilst the latter appeals to matter.

Scathing and complaining references to the Scholastic conception of explanation are common in the seventeenth century. They usually go along with recommendations of the alternative corpuscularian conception.[3] Boyle's are by far the lengthiest strictures on explanation by substantial and accidental forms. He explains how substantial forms are taken to be 'in natural bodies the true principles of their properties, and consequently of their operations'. He explains how there is supposed to be 'in every natural body such a thing as a substantial form, from which all its properties and qualities immediately flow'. However, he says,

> I do not remember that either Aristotle himself . . . or any of his followers, has given a solid and intelligible solution of any one phaenomenon of nature by the help of substantial forms; . . . to say, that such an effect proceeds not from this or that quality of the agent, but from its substantial

form . . . would make a rare philosophy, if it were not far more easy than satisfactory: for if it be demanded why jet attracts straws, rhubarb purges choler, snow dazzles the eyes rather than grass etc. to say, that these and the like effects are performed by the substantial forms of the respective bodies, is at best but to tell me what is the agent, not how the effect is wrought . . . . Wherefore I do not think but that natural philosophy, without being for that the more defective, may well enough spare the doctrine of substantial forms as an useless theory. [3. 46-7]

Elsewhere, in explanation of the way 'the schools have of late much amused the world with a way they have got of referring all natural effects to certain entities, that they call real qualities', he says if

it be demanded how snow comes to dazzle the eyes, they will answer, that it is by a quality of whiteness that is in it which makes all very white bodies produce the same effect: and if you ask what this whiteness is, they will tell you no more in substance, than that it is a real entity which denominates the parcel of matter to which it is joined, white; and if you further inquire what this real entity, which they call a quality, is, you will find . . . that they either speak of it much after the same rate that they do of their substantial forms . . . or at least will not explicate it more intelligibly. [3.12-13]

In opposition to this scheme of things Boyle advocates, as we know, mechanical corpuscular explanations:

almost all sorts of qualities, most of which have been by the schools either left unexplicated, or generally referred to I know not what incomprehensible substantial forms, may be produced mechanically; I mean by such corporeal agents, as do not appear either to work otherwise than by virtue of the motion, size, figure, and contrivance of their own parts. [3.13; also 34-5]

As originally intended, the concepts of form and matter were completely relative to each other. They were not two things which might exist apart from each other. Aristotle is anxious to stress this. Aquinas, too, cautions against thinking of accidental forms as being themselves as it were 'insubstantial' substances. This lack of a real distinction between form and matter is not inconsistent with the idea that forms might be causes. An accidental form does not have to be thought of as having some existence independent of a substance in order for it to cause or make that substance have a certain property. Efficient causes, such as the rain which makes or causes the iron to rust, or the sun's heat which makes or causes it to expand, have this independence. But formal causes are not efficient causes. There is a perfectly good sense of 'makes' (even if not of 'causes') in which it may be said that it is its shape that makes some bronze to be a bowl or a statue.

Quite possibly the seventeenth-century Scholastics did, unlike Aristotle or Aquinas, begin to think of substantial and accidental forms as not being completely correlative to matter and substances. Quite possibly they were guilty of seeing formal causality, the causality involved in the hylemorphic doctrine as being akin to efficient causality. But even if they were innocent of these divergences from the original Aristotelian doctrine their corpuscularian opponents certainly attributed to them corrupt views of this sort. Boyle, it is said, had 'no true appreciation' of the traditional doctrine and failed to distinguish it from the views 'held by the shallow self-styled Aristotelians around him' [*Wiener* 596]. He failed to see that the hylemorphic doctrine was 'metaphysical rather than physical'; he rejected the Aristotelian forms 'because he honestly could not find them in his alembics or vacuum-pump' [598]. Indeed in the quotations given above Boyle does describe the view he is arguing against as holding that accidents or accidental forms are quasi-substances, 'real entities'. Like many others at the time he refers to 'real qualities' and 'real accidents'. Descartes had earlier rejected 'real accidents' as being contradictory. '[W]hatever is real', he said, 'can exist separately apart from any other subject'; but whatever can exist separately is substance not an accident' [2.250]. He similarly rejected substantial form on the ground that it is 'some kind of substance joined to matter . . . and which, no less or even more than matter, is really a substance' [(2) 361].

A popular suggestion is that explanations of natural phenomena attributed to the Scholastics are unsatisfactory because they are circular. This certainly was Glanvill's feeling about them:

that *Gravity* is a *quality* whereby an heavy body descends, is an impertinent *Circle*, and teaches nothing . . . . That the *fire* burns by a quality called *heat*; is an empty dry return to the Question . . . . Even to them, that pretend so much to *Science*, the world is circumscrib'd with a *Gyges his ring*; and is *intellectually invisible*. [(1) 171-2]

But this objection is neither the fairest nor the most illuminating that might be made. In *Le Malade Imaginaire* (1673) an appeal is made to a *virtus dormitiva*, a dormitive virtue, as an explanation of the fact that opium is a soporific. Molière (1622-73) quite rightly makes this seem ridiculous. But what is objectionable about it is not that it is circular and that the dormitive virtue is itself nothing more than the property of putting people to sleep. It is no more circular than an explanation in terms of opium's corpuscular constitution. Would it be objected to this that opium's having its corpuscles arranged in a certain way so as to get it to act in certain way on those of a human body is itself nothing more than its putting people to sleep?

The real objection to Scholastic explanation is the one that lies behind Boyle's complaints. The trouble with it is that it is 'far more easy than satisfactory'. It makes 'it very easy to solve all the phenomena of nature in general, but makes men think it impossible to explicate almost any of them in particular'. Given that such explanations really were intended by any of his Scholastic opponents in the way Boyle supposes, the objection to them is that they reproduce at the level of explanation something completely analogous to what is being explained. The appeal to substantial and accidental forms provides the outline of an explanation, but an outline without content. To explain some thing's having a property X by appeal to an accidental form or real quality of X-ness is merely to erect at the theoretical explanatory level an exact counterpart of that single property. To explain it by saying that the property is a part of or follows from the substantial form of things of that kind is to erect at the level of explanation an exact counterpart of a whole Lockean nominal essence.

This mere outline of explanation, empty of significant detail, means a complete lack of economy. Each thing to be explained is given its own explanatory principle. The corpuscularian hypothesis is quite different in this respect. It holds out the promise of explaining all properties and qualities in terms of a small number of properties of insensible corpuscules. Boyle was evidently very conscious of how unimaginably economical the new hypothesis might appear. He is more than once at pains to show that its claims are not wildly implausible. He points out that given corpuscles of various sizes, shapes and motions, a vast number of different combinations and arrangements are possible. We should not small-mindedly think that 'the mechanical principles . . . can never be applied to all the phaenomena of things corporeal'. This would be like thinking that

> by putting together the letters of the alphabet, one may indeed make up all the words to be found in one book, as in *Euclid*, or *Virgil*; or in one language, as Latin, or English; but that they can by no means suffice to supply words to all the books of a great library, much less to all the languages in the world. [4.70-71; also 3.34-5]

It is often said that the rise of the new science in the seventeenth century made the whole Scholastic apparatus of substantial forms, natures, essences, accidental forms and real qualities, redundant and threw them out. In one way this is true. A certain account or understanding of these ideas certainly was rejected. But in another way it is false. The ideas themselves or what lay behind them were not completely rejected. It is rather that they were reinterpreted. Even if nothing further is or can be said, it is not completely empty to suggest that opium puts people to sleep because it has a dormitive virtue. It is not completely pointless to say that gold is malleable because it is of its nature or essence to be so. For to say this is at any rate to claim that these properties really are possessed by opium or gold as such and are not merely accidental features of some few odd samples of these substances. It is to claim that it is because of something about gold or opium that they have these features.

Whatever else they may have rejected, claims such as these are not rejected by Locke and Boyle. They do not deny there is something about opium which puts people to sleep. They do not deny it is in the nature or essence of gold to be malleable. On the contrary, they freely admit this. What is true of Locke and Boyle is that they then go on to argue that it is in corpuscular, mechanical terms that the soporific quality of opium and the nature of gold is to be understood.

The logical positivists of this century tended to ignore the idea of a real essence to which appeal should be made in explanation of the properties of things. Essences or natures were either dismissed or came to be identified with conventional or arbitrary definitions of words. Though Locke is not to be aligned with this movement of thought he is perhaps partially responsible for it. Unlike Boyle he never attacks the doctrine of substantial forms directly as a conception of explanation. However, the doctrine is connected also with the idea of real definition. We saw in section 8 that Locke attacks this. Later philosophy seems to have confused the rejection of Aristotelian real definitions with the idea that there is nothing to be said for any conception of a real essence or nature. Yet increasingly in the second half of the twentieth century there has been sympathy for and much discussion of real essence.[4]

Notes

[1] Galileo Galilei (1564-1642), an Italian mathematician, astronomer and physicist, developed corpuscularianism in *Il Saggiatiore* (1623). Thomas Hobbes (1588-1679), most famous as a political philosopher for his *Leviathan* (1651), was part of the 'modern' movement but was never accepted by the Royal Society because of his atheism.

[2] For example 'Considerations and Experiments touching the Origin of Forms and Qualities' in *The Origin of Forms and Qualities* [3.14 ff.] and 'The Excellency and Grounds of the Mechanical Hypothesis' in *The Excellency of Theology compared with Natural Philosophy* [4.67 ff.].

[3] *Descartes* (1) 1.295; *Norris* 2.88, 250. For a good account of the rise of the mechanical philosophy and of the demise of scholastic forms see M.B. Hall, 'The Machinery of Nature', *The Makings of Modern Science*, ed. A.R. Hall (Leicester University Press, Leicester, 1960).

[4] See, for example, S. Kripke, *Naming and Necessity* (Harvard University Press, Cambridge, Mass., 1980); H. Putnam, 'Is Semantics Possible?', *Mind, Language and Reality* (Cambridge University Press, Cambridge, 1975).

13 Substances and Substance

Section 11 explained substances, one of the sorts of complex idea that Locke distinguishes. Section 12 followed up in detail one topic which emerged from this explanation. Before we turn to modes, another sort of complex idea, one further thing about substances needs to be considered.

We saw in section 11 that in Locke's extended discussions substance-ideas are ideas of natural kinds of thing which have the properties characteristic of that kind because the corpuscles of matter which make them up are arranged in a certain way. As ideas of natural kinds of thing Locke's substance-ideas are related to Aristotelian second substances. But at the beginning of section 11 we also saw that when Locke first defines them substance-ideas are more like ideas of Aristotelian first substances, ideas of particular individuals. The definition is at II.xii.6. Ideas of substances are 'such combinations of simple Ideas, as are taken to represent distinct particular things subsisting by themselves; in which the supposed, or confused Idea of Substance, such as it is, is always the first and chief'. So far nothing has been said about the confused idea of Substance which appears towards the end of this quotation, and which is supposed to form part of a substance-idea. Even though Locke says relatively little about it it has provoked much discussion both then and since.

This same idea of 'Substance' is referred to elsewhere as 'pure substance in general' [II.xxiii.2], 'matter' [II.xxiii.5, (1) 3], and 'substratum' [II.xxiii.1, 5, IV. vi.7]. The first brief mention of it in II.xii is not developed there. For more about it we must go to II.xxiii which is Locke's first extended treatment of 'Our Complex Ideas of Substances'. There has been one very popular and common interpretation of the opening sections of this chapter. It explains Locke's idea of a 'Substance' or 'substratum' which supposedly forms a part of substance-ideas, as follows.

Blackness and sleekness are accidents. So if we are told that
on the mat there is something that is black and sleek we might
ask what it is. 'A cat' seems to answer this, for cats are substances, individual particular things which have accidents or
properties. But perhaps the answer is not ultimately satisfactory. To say that there is a cat on the mat is surely only to say
that there is something there that is black, sleek, furry, and so
on. But these are all simply accidents. So beyond the answer 'a
cat' there must be something to which they belong. Locke
seems to be thinking along these lines when in speaking of the
qualities we 'find united in the thing called *Horse* or *Stone*' he
says 'we cannot conceive, how they should subsist alone, nor
one in another, [and so] we suppose them existing in, and
supported by some common subject; which Support we denote
by the name Substance' [II.xxiii.4]. This line of thought
suggests that there is a *substratum* to the cat and, of course, to any
other particular thing. We began by speaking of blackness and
sleekness as being accidents of a cat. But we were led to think of
a '*substratum*' underlying these and the other properties of the
cat. So a *substratum* does not, in the ordinary way, *have* properties
which belong to it as they might belong to a cat. Rather it
supports them and they *inhere* in it. We were able in the first place
to think of the cat as having properties, as being an individual
substance, because the idea of a cat is a substance-idea and
hence, so Locke tells us, contains the idea of a *substratum* as one
of its parts.

Is this conclusion about a bare *substratum* underlying all the
properties or accidents of a thing acceptable? Many philosophers, from Isaac Watts and David Hume in the eighteenth
century to Bertrand Russell and A.J. Ayer in the twentieth, say
it is not. According to them a thing is not something, a *substratum*, 'over and above' its qualities but is simply, in Russell's
words, 'a bundle of coexisting qualities'. The idea that properties need an 'unknown *Substance* or subject which supports
them' is, says Watts, 'a meer Mistake', a delusion which arises
from 'our *grammatical* Way of talking by *Substantives* and *Adjec-
tives*'. 'It happens to be the case', says Ayer, 'that we cannot, in
our language, refer to the sensible properties of a thing without
introducing a word or phrase which appears to stand for the

thing itself as opposed to anything which may be said about it'.[1]

It is naturally tempting to think that one of these views must be right. It seems obvious that things either are or else are not simply bundles of properties. But there is no need to decide about this here.[2] All we need note is that the first view, that an individual substance has, over and above its properties and qualities, a *substratum*, has been so closely associated with Locke that there is a tradition of calling it 'the Lockean view of substance'. Recently, however, there has been a tendency to argue that Locke does not hold it at all. It is not suggested that he holds the contrary view – though Stillingfleet did accuse him of 'almost discarding substance out of the reasonable part of the world' [*Locke* (5) 4.7-8]. The idea is rather that Locke was not interested in logical questions about substance and accidents and that his talk of a *substratum* is not an answer to them. We should not exaggerate Locke's lack of interest in these questions. They certainly sometimes seem in his mind when he writes to Stillingfleet [(5) 4.8]. But the tradition that finds in the *Essay* 'the Lockean view of substance' no doubt distorts the overall shape of his thought and misfocusses attention.

An indication of the real direction of Locke's interest in his talk about *substratum* is given by the observation that it is only *some* of a substance's properties which are supposed by Locke to subsist in its *substratum* [*Bolton* 494]. These would not include, in the case of gold, being valuable or being used as a monetary standard. They would include its being yellow and its being fusible. The properties which are supposed to subsist in a *substratum* are, in short, only those which may be supposed to result from the arrangement of the corpuscles of the matter constituting the substance.

So according to recent suggestions we should not interpret Locke's talk of a *substratum* primarily in terms of a logical question about the relation between substances and any of their accidents or properties. Rather we should understand it in terms of the corpuscular account of matter which provides an explanation of these properties of substances in which a natural philosopher might be interested. Accordingly, Locke's references to 'Substance' are not so much to a featureless *substratum* as to the 'catholick or universal' matter of Boyle's corpuscular hypothesis. This idea of there being a connexion between a substance's *substratum* and corpuscular matter has been developed in various ways.[3] But there is no need for us to go into its detail. Rather we should now move from relations (section 10) and substances (sections 11, 12, and 13) to the third sort of complex idea which Locke distinguishes, ideas of modes.

Notes

[1] A.J. Ayer, *Language, Truth and Logic* (Gollancz, London, 2nd. edn. 1946), p.42; David Hume, *Treatise of Human Nature* (1739), I.i.6; Bertrand Russell, *Inquiry into Meaning and Truth* (Allen and Unwin, London, 1940), p.97; Isaac Watts, *Logick; or, The right use of Reason* (1725), p.13.

[2] See my *Locke's Philosophy of Science and Knowledge* (Blackwell, Oxford, 1971), pp.68 ff.

[3] P. Alexander, 'Locke on Substance-in-General', *Ratio*, 22 (1980), 23 (1981); M. Ayers, 'The Ideas of Power and Substance in Locke's Philosophy', *Philosophical Quarterly*, 25 (1975); *Bolton*; *Mackie* 76 ff.; M. Mandelbaum, *Philosophy, Science and Sense Perception* (Johns Hopkins Press, Baltimore, 1964), pp.37 ff.

14 Modes (and Substances)

In fact there are two sorts of mode, *simple* and *mixed*. Simple modes are 'variations, or different combinations of the same simple Idea, without the mixture of any other, as a dozen, or score; which are nothing but the Ideas of so many distinct Unites added together' [II.xii.5]. Mixed modes are 'compounded of simple Ideas of several kinds, put together to make one complex one; v.g. Beauty, consisting of a certain composition of Colour and Figure, causing delight in the Beholder' [II.xii.5]. Often the distinction between them is not taken to be important, and reference is made simply to 'modes' [II.xxxi.3, 14].

Simple modes are 'variations or different combinations' of the same idea. It is not clear whether 'variation' and 'combination' are meant to be two things or just stylistic variants on one. But Locke does treat simple modes in two different ways which could plausibly be related to these two phrases. In one place we are told that 'by putting twelve Unites together, we have the complex Idea of a dozen; and so of a Score, or a Million, or any other Number' [II.xvi.2]. It was suggested in section 6 that it is a mistake to think in this way of the idea of a dozen as being twelve ideas of a single thing rather than as being a single idea of twelve things. Whether or not it is a mistake, this case of number does illustrate the idea of 'different combinations of the same idea'. Talk of 'variations', on the other hand, is given content by a different range of cases. These are ones where the relation between simple modes and simple ideas is akin to that between determinates and determinables. A good example of this is the suggestion that 'To slide, roll, tumble, walk, creep, run, dance, leap, skip . . . are all but the different modifications of Motion' [II.xviii 2].

Most of what Locke says about modes contrasts them, explicitly and implicitly, with substance-ideas. These last are ideas of natural kinds of material things which have the properties and characteristics of that kind because their constituent corpuscles are arranged in a certain way. Whereas modes are 'Combinations . . . not looked upon to be the characteristical Marks of any real Beings that have a steady existence, but scattered and independent Ideas, put together by the Mind'. In this they 'are thereby distinguished from the complex Ideas of Substances' [II.xxii.1,2]. Unlike substance-ideas they are their own 'archetypes' [II.xxxi.3, 14]. They are 'voluntary collections' [II.xxxi. 3, 6] of 'scattered and independent Ideas' [II.xxii.1, III.v.3,6] which are 'made by the mind' [II.xxii.1,2, xxxi.3]. They are 'creatures of the understanding' [III.v.12]. Unlike substance-ideas which are 'Works of Nature' [III.v.12] whose component ideas 'have an Union in Nature' [III.v.11].

So what are modes exactly? They certainly are *not* ideas of material things. They do not, we may remember from the beginning of section 11, have the idea of *substratum* as one of their parts. This means they have no corpuscular constitution and, as a consequence, there will be no explanation in terms of a corpuscular real essence of why they have the particular properties they do. This is at least part of what is meant by the component ideas of a mode being scattered, independent, and having no unity in nature.

If modes have no unity in nature, why do 'Men . . . make several Combinations of simple Ideas into distinct, and . . . settled Modes, and neglect others, which in the Nature of Things themselves, have as much aptness to be combined' [II.xxii.5]? It is because they 'usually make such Collections of Ideas into complex Modes . . . as they have frequent use of in their way of Living and Conversation, leaving others, which they have but seldom an occasion to mention, loose and without names' [II.xxii.5]. We should understand from this that modes are conventional or institutional. Indeed Locke says that 'to enumerate all the mixed Modes . . . would be to make a Dictionary of the greatest part of the Words made use of in Divinity, Ethicks, Law, and Politicks' [II.xxii.12]. The examples 'obligation', 'lie', 'hypocrisy', 'sacrilege', 'murder', 'parricide', obviously come from these institutional areas [II.xxii. 1, 2, 3, 4,

12]. The conventional nature of modes is often stressed. 'Languages constantly change, take up new, and lay by old terms . . . [b]ecause change of Customs and Opinions bring[s] . . . with it new Combinations of Ideas' [II.xxii.7]. Often there are 'Words in one Language, which have not any that answer them in another' [III.v.8]. All of this 'could not have happened, if these Species were the steady Workmanship of Nature; and not Collections made and abstracted by the Mind, in order to naming, and for the convenience of Communication' [III.v.8].

Modes, then, are conventional and have no 'Union in Nature'. There is no explanation in terms of a corpuscular real essence why they are as they are. This does not mean that their parts are not connected and unified. They are joined together and unified by the mind and by the fact of there being a word in the language for them:

> the connexion between the loose parts of those complex Ideas, being made by the Mind, this union, which has no particular foundation in Nature, would cease again, were there not something that did, as it were, hold it together, and keep the parts from scattering. Though therefore it be the Mind that makes the Collection, 'tis the Name which is as it were the Knot, that ties them fast together. [III.v.10]

What does Locke mean by the mind and a name collecting and tying together the parts of a mode? Perhaps he is thinking of the conditions under which we would say that a certain mode exists. Perhaps he is suggesting that the existence of a certain mode consists solely in people having the idea and a word for it. It is clear that the existence of a substance such as gold does not simply consist in people having the idea of, and a word for it. Gold exists quite independently of people recognising its existence and having a name for it. It is not so clear that the same goes for conventional and institutional modes like marriage and obligation. In a society where marriage is not recognised is there nevertheless such a thing as marriage? This difference reflects the point made at the beginning of section 10 that the distinction between an idea and what the idea is an idea of is not sharp in the case of modes but is in the case of substances. It seems to be what Locke has in mind when he says that modes have no reality other than what they have in the minds of men and are appropriately called 'notions' [II.xxii.2, xxx.4, III. v.12].

A further difference between modes and substances is that 'in the Species of . . . Modes . . . [real and nominal essences] are always the same: But in Substances, always quite different' [III.iii.18, v.14]. From the point of view of Locke's avowed purpose in the *Essay* to investigate the origin, certainty, and extent of knowledge this contrast is easily the most important. We should deal with it at some length.

Sections 11 to 13 showed how to understand the notions of real and nominal essence in connexion with substances. Substances are kinds of naturally occurring thing or stuff. Their nominal essences, which may differ from person to person, have to do with how we pick out, describe, and characterise them. The nominal essence of gold has to do with its observable characteristics such as its yellowness, malleability, and solubility in *aqua regia*. The real essences of substances are, however, those arrangements of corpuscles of the matter which constitute them which explain or account for the properties listed in the nominal essences. If we knew the real essence of gold, as perhaps God and the angels do, then that is how we would pick it out and characterise it. In this case real and nominal essence would coincide. As things stand, however, they do not. Real and nominal essences are 'in Substances, always quite different'.

But how are we to understand the notions of real and nominal essence in connexion with modes? How are we to understand Locke's statement that these coincide? It is easy to see what a mode's nominal essence is. It has to do with what we mean by the mode's name. It has to do with what we mean by the idea we have of that particular mode. But what is a mode's real essence? It seems clear that it cannot be a corpuscular constitution as it is in the case of a substance. Should we then conclude that modes have no real essence? Locke certainly did not draw this conclusion. The idea that modes do indeed have real essences plays a crucial part in his theory of knowledge. But even if Locke does think that modes have real essences it is far from clear that he *should* think so, and commentators have shown a marked tendency to be sceptical about the application to modes of the idea of a real essence.

Some commentators seem to deny that Locke's modes are even *supposed* to have real essences. 'A substance has a real essence which makes a unity of the properties which constitute it . . . [a] mode has no real essence which makes a unity of the properties which constitute it'.[1] Apparently this says that modes have no real essence for Locke. But this is simply false. After all, we are considering Locke's suggestion that 'the names of mixed modes always signify . . . the real essence of their species'. This clearly presupposes that modes do have real essences. Indeed there are many other passages in which Locke speaks of the real essences of modes [III.v.14; also II.xxxii.24, III.iii.18, xi.15, IV.xii.7-9, vi.4]. Perhaps these commentators do no really deny that Locke's modes have no real essence. Perhaps what was meant was that though modes do have real essences for Locke they have no real essence of a kind which makes a unity of properties. But this is no better. One difficulty with it is that real essences just are things which make a unity of properties. They are that 'on which all the properties of the Species depend, and from which alone they all flow' [III.v.14], they are 'that Foundation from which all . . . Properties [of the species] flow' [III.iii.18]. There simply are not two sorts of real essence, those which do and those which do not make a unity of properties. Something which does not make a unity of properties is not just one particular kind of real essence. It is no real essence at all. A second and associated difficulty with this interpretation of Locke is that we shall shortly come to passages where Locke clearly implies that modal real essences unify properties.

Other commentators too have been sceptical about modal real essences. Jonathan Bennett does not deny that Locke's modes are *supposed* to have real essences. But he does say that the distinction between real essence and nominal essence does not work in their case and 'works only in application to substances' [123]. He says that Locke records this 'not very satisfactorily, by saying that the nominal essence of a . . . mode is also its real essence'. We shall see that Bennett could be right that the distinction does *not* work very well for modes. But the fact that it doesn't has nothing whatsoever to do with Locke's view that the two modal essences coincide. In expressing this view Locke is not expressing, leave alone recording, unease about the notion of a modal real essence. J.L. Mackie does not go so far as to say that Locke sees that the distinction between real and nominal essence does not work for modes. But he does say that it is 'of little importance' [89]. His reason is Locke's view that the two sorts of essence coincide.

But a distinction can be important and undeniable even if its two sides happen in fact to coincide. The undeniable distinction between the left-hand side of the road and the side on which one must·drive does not disappear in England where the two sides happen to be the same. It must be insisted against Bennett and Mackie that for Locke the notions of real and nominal essence and the distinction between them are as important with modes as with substances. Modal real and nominal essences coincide, but this does not mean that the distinction is unimportant, much less that it is a failure.

But is the idea of modal real essence actually consistent with other things Locke says about modes? We have already noted him saying that modes are composed of 'scattered and independent Ideas' which have no 'Union in Nature'. We understood him to mean simply that they have no *corpuscular* real essence. But when one also remembers the conventionality he attributes to them and the fact that it is the mind and language that 'keep the parts from scattering' one might begin to wonder. Something with a real essence is surely a united whole with an integrated mind-independent coherence. Locke seems to deny that modes are like this, and so, one might perhaps be forgiven for concluding, they have no real essence.

The fact of the matter is, I think, that Locke is not entirely consistent. Much of what he says about modes does *not* go well with the idea that they have real essences just as much as substances do. Nevertheless he *does* have that idea. It is crucial and central to his explanation why geometry exists as a science, as a body of *a priori* knowledge, and why natural philosophy does not. Even if he says things inconsistent with this idea we must not be blinded to the fact that he has it, and that it is important to his overall scheme.

But even if there were no question of inconsistency here, there could be a further reason why someone might feel uneasy about modal real essence or attribute unease about it to Locke. It stems from the simple fact that modes are not substances. Modal real essences can hardly be *just like* substantial real essences. They can hardly be arrangements of corpuscles moving in accordance with the laws of mechanics. But this does not mean that there are no such things. We saw in section 12 that the notion of a substantial real essence is one thing, and Locke's own particular interpretation of it as a corpuscular constitution is another. A similar point can be made here. The notion of a real essence is one thing. It is 'that Foundation from which all . . . Properties [of the species] flow' [III.iii.18]. An account of substantial real essence is another. It is merely a particular application of this general idea of real essence. Modes do not have corpuscular real essences but this does not of itself mean that they have no real essence at all.

How exactly, then, does Locke seek to apply the notion of real essence to modes? In section 11 we looked at its application to substances in the light of a distinction analogous to that between the observable properties of the Strasbourg cathedral clock and its inner mechanism. The general point was made there that for the notion of a real essence to have a place one needs to be able to distinguish between characteristic observable features and what produces, accounts for, or explains them. Can such a distinction be made for modes? It is plain from the following passage that Locke thinks it can:

> Figure including a Space between three Lines, is the real, as well as nominal Essence of a Triangle; it being not only the abstract Idea to which the general Name is annexed, but the very *Essentia*, or Being, of the thing it self, that Foundation from which all its Properties flow, and to which they are all inseparably annexed. But it is far otherwise concerning that parcel of Matter, which makes the Ring on my Finger, wherein these two Essences are apparently different. For it is the real Constitution of its insensible Parts, on which depend all those Properties of Colour, Weight, Fusibility, Fixedness, *etc.* which are to be found in it. Which Constitution we know not; and so having no particular Idea of, have no Name that is the Sign of it. But yet it is its Colour, Weight, Fusibility, and Fixedness, *etc.* which makes it to be Gold, or gives it a right to that Name, which is therefore its nominal Essence. [III.iii.18; also II. xxxi.6, xxxii.24]

This passage makes clear, at least in general terms, how

Locke intends there to be a parallel between modes such as triangles on the one hand, and gold and the Strasbourg clock on the other. In the passage modes *are* thought of as having a real essence which makes a unity of their properties. A clock with a certain mechanism will, as a consequence of having that mechanism, put on a certain outward show. Some matter with corpuscles of a certain size, shape, and arrangement, will have certain resultant properties. Similarly a figure of three lines including a space will, as a consequence of being constructed in this way, have internal angles equal to two right angles and external angles larger than internal opposites [IV.vi.10, viii.8].

The parallel is attractive and plausible. There is a clear and workable distinction between the characteristic features of a triangle (and of other geometrical figures) and what accounts for or explains them. To begin with, triangles do have a number of characteristic properties [II. xxxi.6, 10, xxxii.24]. For example, their internal angles are equal to two right angles and their external angles are larger than their internal opposites. It is plausible moreover to suppose that they have these properties as a result of their real essence. H.W.B. Joseph suggests that we might think of a real essence as serving 'to set the subject before us'. It is that 'with which we must start, in order to have the figure before us, and say anything about it'.[2] We might think of it as a specification, as a blueprint, or set of instructions for constructing a certain figure. A figure of 'three lines including a Space' [II.xxxii.24], or 'a Figure, with three sides meeting at three Angles' [II.xxxi.3], which Locke gives as the real essence of a triangle does seem to be one such specification. Furthermore, when a figure is drawn according to it, it will be found to have and by a geometer might have been predicted to have the characteristic properties mentioned above.

It appears then that we can distinguish the real essence of a triangle from the properties a figure will have as a result of having this real essence. Our own ideas are in fact of this real essence. They are not formed merely 'by collecting . . . Properties' [II.xxxi.11; also 10, xxxii.24]. A figure of 'three Lines including a Space' is a real essence which tells us what a triangle is. It can be distinguished from the properties which a figure will have when it is constructed according to this essence. The distinction can be made in the case of the circle too. Circles are figures which bear a constant relation to one point. Knowledge of this real essence enables us to construct a circle; for example by revolving a pencil on a fixed arm around a fixed point. As a result of being figures which bear a constant relation to one point circles have a number of characteristic properties. For example, equal chords subtend equal angles on their circumferences. Locke discusses the ellipse in these terms at II.xxxi. 10-11, and distinguishes the real essence from the properties to which it gives rise.

This general distinction between a real essence and the properties it gives rise to is crucial for what Locke says 'Of Adequate and Inadequate Ideas' [II.xxxi] – a topic postponed from section 6. An idea of gold which is in terms of its outer observable characteristics and properties such as its colour or its malleability will be inadequate. Gold has many properties other than these and no person's idea will capture them all. '['T]is probable, if anyone knew all the Properties, that are by divers Men known of this Metal, there would be an hundred times as many . . . go to the complex Idea of Gold, as any one Man yet has in his; and yet, perhaps, that not be the thousandth part of what is to be discovered in it' [II.xxxi.10]. On the other hand, however, an idea in terms of gold's real essence or corpuscular constitution will be adequate. In having a grasp of what gives rise to all of gold's properties one would, so to speak, grasp all those properties themselves. On the basis of the idea of a real essence we could 'grasp at a time whole Sheaves [of properties]; and in bundles, comprehend the Nature and Properties of whole Species together' [IV.xii.12].

Our ideas of substances are imperfect and inadequate because we do not know their real essences. Our ideas of them have to do merely with a collection of their properties. What then of modes such as geometrical figures? There would be imperfection and inadequacy here too 'if we were to have our complex Ideas of them, only by collecting their Properties . . . . How uncertain, and imperfect, would our Ideas be of an Ellipsis, if we had no other Idea of it, but some few of its Properties?' [II.xxxi.10]. But our ideas of these figures are *not* formed by 'collecting' their properties. We know their real essences and so our ideas of them are perfect and adequate. '[B]y having the Idea of a Figure, with three sides meeting at three Angles, I have a complete Idea, wherein I require nothing else to make it perfect' [II.xxxi.3]. In this case we can 'comprehend the Nature and Properties of whole Species together' for 'having in our plain Ideas, the whole Essence of that Figure, we from thence discover those Properties, and demonstratively see how they flow, and are inseparable from it' [II.xxxi.11].

The idea that in the cases both of substances and of modes a distinction can be drawn between a real essence and properties which flow from it is attractive and plausible. But there are some difficulties and blemishes in it. The distinction between a corpuscular constitution and the properties which 'flow from' it is hardly arbitrary. Properties such as its colour, its malleability, its solubility in certain acids, are clearly not part of gold's corpuscular essence. It is clear that they are rather to be accounted for and explained by reference to that real essence. But is the distinction between the real essence of a geometrical figure and the properties which are dependent on it so clearcut? Hasn't it a measure of arbitrariness? People often suggest that we can construct a triangle not only from *Locke's* specification of a figure of 'three Lines including a Space', but just as easily also from the different specification of 'a figure the sum of whose angles is two right-angles'.[3] According to Locke this second specification gives not a real essence but merely a property which flows from a real essence. But *if* the distinction is arbitrary we have no reason to say with him that the first is 'a more compleat or perfect Idea' than the second [II.xxxi.3].

There is a further difficulty for the parallel between substances and modes. We have just observed that the distinction between the characteristic features of a geometrical figure and what accounts for or explains them may not be as clear as at first appeared. In other modal cases the distinction runs into difficulty even sooner. If we reflect on justice, gratitude and courage we might feel that it can be made [II.xxx.4, III.v.12]. We might say of someone's idea or conception of justice or courage that it is superficial, limited to the outer appearances or manifestations of these things, or tied to a small range of particular cases. Someone may, for example, be unable to see how courage can be shown in circumstances other than those of purely physical danger. He may be unable to see what it might be to be *morally* courageous. And this seems to provide a foothold for the thought that there is a distinction to be made between the essences and the external characteristics and properties of justice and courage. But it is very difficult to see a foothold for this thought in the cases of drunkenness, procession, and parricide [II.xxii.1, 4, III.v.13]. What would it be to have a merely superficial conception of these things?

The discussion of the last page or so began with the question how we are to understand Locke's statement that 'in the Species of . . . Modes . . . [real and nominal essences] are always the same: But in Substances, always quite different'. The answer should now be clear. There is a coincidence between nominal and real essence when *our* idea of a certain kind of thing, what we mean by the name of that kind, is in fact an idea of the real essence of that kind. Our ideas of substances are inadequate and confined to some few of their observable characteristics and properties. We are ignorant of the details of the corpuscular constitutions which give rise to these properties. So the nominal essence of a substance does not coincide with its real essence. On the other hand, our ideas of modes are adequate. They capture real essences, not merely a small collection of resultant properties. So it is that 'in the species of modes real and nominal essences are the same'.

So far as our ideas of them go the dfference between modes and substances comes down to this. Just as an horologist knows the real essence of a Strasbourg-type clock so we know the real essence of geometrical figures and of other modes. However, just as a gazing countryman does not know the real essence of a Strasbourg-type clock so we do not know the real essence of gold and of other substances. This difference between modes and substances is of crucial importance for Locke's basic question about the limits and extent of knowledge. How this is so will be considered in the next section.

Notes

[1] C. Aronson, D. Lewis, 'Locke on Mixed Modes, Knowledge, and Substances', *Journal of the History of Philosophy*, 8 (1970), p.195; also 196, 197.

[2] *Introduction to Logic*, 2nd. edn. (Oxford University, Oxford, 1916), p.99.

[3] R.R. Macleod, 'Professor Ritchie on Essence in Geometry', *Mind* 65 (1956).

15   The Extent and Limits of Knowledge

In section 9 we found the beginning of Locke's answer to his question about the limits and extent of knowledge. One important limit was that it did not extend into 'natural philosophy'. We cannot have knowledge of the properties and powers of substances such as gold, because there are no necessary connexions visible between the relevant ideas. Unlike the study of triangles and other geometrical figures, the study of gold has to be by way of observation and experiment. It was appropriate to ask at this point why knowledge has this particular boundary. Why is there a 'want of discoverable connexion between those ideas we have' in these cases? Why do some ideas have 'discoverable connexions' between them and others do not? At the very end of section 9 the outline of answers to these questions was given. In brief it was this. We can discern necessary connexions between our ideas in geometry and ethics, and progress by reasoning and abstract thought, because these subjects concern modes whose real essences we know. But natural philosophy has to do with substances whose real essences we do not know. This is why it is an experimental, observational subject. Since sections 10 to 14 have discussed the distinction between modes and substances and the notion of real essence we are now in a position to look in more detail at Locke's conclusions about the extent of knowledge.

Locke first expresses these ideas about how the extent of knowledge proper depends on our knowledge of real essence at III.v.14. He begins by saying that *'the Names of mixed Modes always signifie . . . the real Essences of their Species'*. He then continues, 'and so in these the *real* and *nominal Essence* is the same; which of what Concernment it is to the certain Knowledge of general Truths, we shall see hereafter'. What we do see 'hereafter' is that 'natural Philosophy is not capable of being made a Science' [IV.xii.10] because we do not know substantial real essences and our substance-ideas are inadequate. We see also that geometry *is* capable of demonstration because it deals with adequate ideas of modes whose real essences we do know. This difference between natural science and mathematics comes out well in this passage:

> The complex Ideas we have of Substances, are . . . Collections of simple Ideas . . . . But such a complex Idea cannot be the real Essence of any Substance; for then the Properties we discover in that Body, would depend on that complex Idea, and be deducible from it, and their necessary connexion with it be known; as all Properties of a Triangle depend on, and as far as they are discoverable, are deducible from the complex Idea of three Lines including a Space. [II.xxxi.6]

Locke emphasises more how we have little knowledge about substances because we do *not* know their real essences, than how we have knowledge about modes because we *do* know theirs. But these two sides of the single idea that the possibility of genuine certain knowledge as opposed to merely probable opinion has to do with our knowing real essences, come nicely together at IV.xii. 7-10. We must, Locke says, 'adapt our methods of Enquiry to the nature of the Ideas we examine, and the Truth we search after'. He clearly has in mind that the coincidence or otherwise of nominal and real essence determines what we can hope to know and how we can hope to know it. In mathematics where we know real essences, we can attain 'certain, real, and general Truths' by the *a priori* methods of intuition or demonstration. Similarly, 'if other Ideas, that are the real, as well as nominal Essences of their Species, were pursued in the way familiar to Mathematicians, they would carry our Thoughts farther, and with greater evidence and clearness than possibly we are apt to imagine'. So it is that Locke suggests that 'Morality is capable of Demonstration, as well as Mathematicks' for 'the Ideas that Ethicks are conversant about [are] . . . all real Essences'. In natural philosophy, however, the nominal essences of substances are different from their real essences which do not know. As a result we can demonstrate nothing and achieve little general knowledge, little certainty:

In our search after the Knowledge of Substances, our want of Ideas, that are suitable to such a way of proceeding, obliges us to a quite different method. We advance not here, as in the other (where our abstract Ideas are real as well as nominal Essences) by contemplating our Ideas . . . . By which, I think, it is evident, that Substances afford Matter of very little general Knowledge; and the bare Contemplation of their abstract Ideas, will carry us but a very little way in the search of Truth and Certainty . . . . [T]he want of Ideas of their real Essences sends us from our own Thoughts, to the Things themselves, as they exist. *Experience here must teach me*, what Reason cannot: and 'tis by trying alone, that I can certainly know, what other Qualities co-exist with those of my complex *Idea*, v.g. whether that yellow, heavy, fusible Body, I call Gold, be malleable, or no; which Experience . . . makes me not certain, that it is so, in all, or any other yellow, heavy, fusible Bodies, but that which I have tried . . . . Because the other Properties of such Bodies, depending not on these, but on that unknown real Essence, on which these also depend, we cannot by them discover the rest. [IV.xii.9]

In section 9 we saw that Locke's distinction between knowledge and opinion is, in effect, the more recent distinction between *a priori* and *a posteriori* knowledge. Now, at least in the twentieth century, many philosophers have supposed that all *a priori* knowledge is trifling and empty of content. By contrast with *a posteriori* knowledge it is not really worth having. There has been a tendency to suppose that the price paid for the certainty of *a priori* knowledge is a loss of information. It needs to be stressed that Locke does not share this tendency. He would agree, to be sure, that *some* of our certain knowledge is trifling and uninformative. He would agree that *some* propositions are merely analytic and lacking in content. But he would not agree that all are. For he makes a distinction between two sorts of proposition which we can know with certainty. He calls them *trifling* and *instructive*. His view is that the *a priori* certain knowledge he discusses in mathematics and ethics is not trifling and analytic, but informative. But is Locke justified in thinking that *a priori* certain knowledge is not inevitably trifling and uninformative? Does he have any grounds or arguments for thinking this? At least one commentator is sure he does not. He says there is an 'important and fundamental weakness in Locke's account of general knowledge'. This is the 'unexamined conviction that we can apprehend necessary instructive agreements and disagreements between concepts'. There is 'little difficulty in appreciating the necessary truth of trifling propositions, but we must view as problematic at best the purported necessity of instructive propositions . . . . Locke evidently recognised no problem in this regard; at least he proposed no solution' [*Perry* 234-5].

These objections to Locke are misplaced. His distinction between triflingly certain and instructively certain knowledge is no more of a problem than that between real essence and resulting properties, a distinction with which it is closely connected. Both sorts of certain knowledge arise from the perception of necessary connexions between ideas. If this necessary connexion results from the *containment* of one idea by another then there is trifling certainty. An instructive certainty, however, results from one idea being a necessary but non-contained consequence of another:

> We can know then the Truth of two sorts of Propositions, with perfect certainty; the one is of those trifling Propositions, which have a certainty in them, but 'tis a verbal Certainty, but not instructive. And, secondly, we can know the Truth, and so may be certain in Propositions, which affirm something of another, which is a necessary consequence of its precise complex Idea, but not contained in it. As that the external Angle of all Triangles, is bigger than either of the opposite internal Angles; which relation of the outward Angle, to either of the opposite internal Angles, making no part of the complex Idea, signified by the name Triangle, this is a real Truth, and conveys with it instructive real knowledge. [IV.viii.8]

What exactly is this distinction between one idea being necessarily connected with another because contained in it, and one idea being a necessary but non-contained consequence of another? We should understand it as follows.

We can distinguish between the real essence or corpuscular constitution of gold and its consequent malleability and fusibility. But our idea of gold is not of this real essence which we do not know. It is of a collection of ideas such as those of malleability, fusibility, and so on. This means that the ideas of malleability and fusiblity are *contained* in our idea of gold. We can distinguish, too, between the real essence of a triangle, 'a figure of three lines enclosing a space', and consequent properties such as having angles equal to two right angles. Since we know the real essence of a triangle our idea is of it. It is not merely of the various properties which flow from that real essence. This means that the ideas of these properties are *not contained* in our idea of a triangle – though of course they are nevertheless a necessary consequence of it.

This understanding of the difference between one idea being necessarily connected with another because contained in it, and an idea being a necessary but non-contained consequence of another, enables us to understand the distinction between trifling and instructive certainties. Our knowledge that triangles have angles equal to two right angles is instructively certain. It is certain because the idea of having angles of that size is a necessary consequence of our idea of a triangle, for having angles of that size flows from the real essence of which our idea is. It is instructive because the one idea is not contained in the other. Our knowledge that gold is malleable is triflingly certain [III.vi.50, IV.vi.90]. It is certain because the idea of malleability is a necessary consequence of our idea of gold, for it is a part of it. It is trifling because the one idea is a part of and so contained in the other. If we knew the real essence of gold and our nominal essence, our idea of it, were of a stuff internally constituted of corpuscles of a certain size and shape we would then have *instructively* certain knowledge of gold's malleability. It would be certain because the idea of malleability would be a necessary consequence of our idea of gold, for malleability flows from the real essence of which our idea would then be. It would be instructive because the idea of malleability would as before, be non-contained in our idea of gold.

So we see that Locke would not go along with the twentieth-century tendency of supposing that *a priori* knowledge is inevitably trifling and empty of content. There is a further important respect in which what he says about knowledge and opinion diverges from what would be accepted in this century. We have no knowledge proper, no *a priori* knowledge, in natural science. We can discern no necessary connexions there. But is this because there are no necessary connexions to be perceived, or is it because we cannot perceive connexions that are nevertheless there? Since Hume in the eighteenth century many people would assert the first of these alternatives. But Locke would assert the second. In natural philosophy 'Experience must teach me, what Reason cannot'. The methods and procedures of natural philosophy are different from those of mathematics. But for Locke this is not because there is no knowledge proper to be had in this area. Rather it is because *we* cannot attain it; and we cannot do so because we do not know substantial real essences. If we *did* know them then we *could* proceed in an *a priori* fashion and *would* have knowledge proper. These two important passages make this point:

> if we could discover the Figure, Size, Texture, and Motion of the minute Constituent parts of any two Bodies, we should know without Trial several of their Operations one upon another, as we do now the Properties of a Square, or a Triangle. Did we know the Mechanical affections of the Particles of Rhubarb, Hemlock, Opium, and a Man, as a Watchmaker does those of a Watch, whereby it performs its Operations, and of a File which by rubbing on them will alter the Figure of any of the Wheels, we should be able to tell before Hand, that Rhubarb will purge, Hemlock kill, and Opium make a Man sleep; as well as a Watch-maker can, that a little piece of Paper laid on the Balance, will keep the Watch from going, till it be removed; or that some small part of it, being rubb'd by a File, the Machin would quite lose its Motion, and the Watch go no more. The dissolving of Silver in *aqua fortis*, and Gold in *aqua Regia*, and not *vice versa*, would be then, perhaps, no more difficult to know, than it is to a Smith to understand, why the turning of one Key will open a Lock, and not the turning of another. [IV.iii.25]
>
> Had we such Ideas of Substances, as to know what real Constitutions produce those sensible Qualities we find in them, and how those Qualities flowed from thence, we could, by the specifick Ideas of their real Essences in our own Minds, more certainly find out their Properties, and discover what Qualities they had, or had not, than we can now by our Senses: and to know the Properties of Gold, it would be no more necessary, that Gold should exist, and that we should make Experiments upon it, than it is necessary for the knowing the Properties of a Triangle, that a Triangle should exist in any Matter, the Idea in our Minds would serve for the one, as well as the other. [IV.vi.11]

Natural philosophy lies beyond the limits of human knowledge and certainty for Locke. But this is not because there is, as it were, no knowledge there to be had. Substances do have real essences and if we knew them then natural philosophy could be every bit a true science, every bit as much a systematic body of certain knowledge, as mathematics and geometry.

It is precisely because human knowledge can extend into any area where we have ideas of the relevant real essences that Locke suggests that with due application we could develop a systematic science of ethics similar to mathematics and geometry. For ethical ideas are mixed modes whose real essences we know. In a famous passage he explains that

> The Idea of a supreme Being, infinite in Power, Goodness, and Wisdom, whose Workmanship we are, and on whom we depend; and the Idea of our selves, as understanding, rational Beings, being such as are clear in us, would, I suppose, if duly considered, and pursued, afford such Foundations of our Duty and Rules of Action, as might place *Morality amongst the Sciences capable of Demonstration:* wherein I doubt not, but from self-evident Propositions, by necessary Consequences, as incontestable as those in Mathematicks, the measures of right and wrong might be made out. [IV.iii.18]

The idea of God lies at the foundation of this possible science of morality because morality is, Locke holds, a matter of God's will. Moral law is divine law. 'God has given a Rule whereby Men should govern themselves . . . . This is the only true touchstone of moral Rectitude' [II.xxviii.8; also I.iv.8]. Clearly, however, the science of morality Locke envisages is poorly founded unless we know for certain that God really exists and that we should indeed obey his will. Locke thinks the second of these points is intuitively self-evident. We 'as certainly know that Man is to honour, fear, and obey GOD as . . . that Three, Four, and Seven, are less than Fifteen' [IV.xiii.3]. Knowledge of the actual existence of God depends on demonstration. Where then does our idea of God come from and how do we know that something corresponding to it exists?

Locke allows that if any idea were innate the idea of God would be. But (we saw in section 3) no ideas are, so this is not [I.iv.8, IV.x.1]. Descartes' God created us with an idea of him in our minds as a trademark. Locke's did not. He did however give us the means to construct an idea of him from experience [II.xxiii.33, IV.x.1], the source of all our ideas. Also he provided us with the means, the ability to reason, to have certain knowledge of his existence [IV.x.1].

Locke refers at one point to a demonstration of the existence of God which depends on 'Men's having that Idea of GOD in

their Minds' [IV.x.7]. He gives no more detail than this and it is
generally thought that he has in mind the so-called ontological
proof as put forward by Descartes in the fifth *Meditation*. Very
briefly, this depends on the thought that the idea of existing is a
part of our idea of God just as the idea of having angles equal to
two right angles is part of our idea of a triangle. In a paper
written in 1696 Locke explicitly considers this proof and rejects
it [(4) 313 f.]. In the *Essay* he was not so certain about its
unacceptability. He says only that is is not a good foundation on
which 'to lay the whole stress of so important a Point' as the
existence of God [IV.x.7]. In his later criticism of it Locke
argues that 'any idea . . . barely by being in our minds, is no
evidence of the real existence of anything out of our minds,
answering that idea . . . . [T]he real existence of a God can only
be proved by the real existence of other things' [(4) 316]. The
proof he offers in the *Essay*, apparently under the influence of
Nicole and Ralph Cudworth, accords with this recommenda-
tion.[1] It begins with our intuitive certainty of our own real
existence as intelligent, perceiving, and knowing beings
[IV.x.2,5]. Then, *via* other intuitive certainties, it reaches the
conclusion that we must have been created by a knowing,
intelligent being that existed from eternity [IV.x.5].

One step in Locke's reasoning is that it is impossible that
thinking, intelligent beings should have come about by accident
from some mere chance arrangement of atoms. It is 'as impossible, that Things wholly void of Knowledge, and operating
blindly, and without any Perception, should produce a knowing
Being, as it is impossible, that a Triangle should make it self
three Angles bigger than two right ones' [IV.x.5]. Now we shall
see in section 17 that Locke allows as a possibility that 'some
Systems of Matter fitly disposed' might have 'a power to perceive and think' [IV.iii.6]. He allows, that is, that even though
we have the capacity to think and perceive we might be wholly
material beings. Locke was told that some of his readers felt he
was not being consistent. He agreed that the passages in question may 'to an unwary reader, seem to contain a contradiction'
[(6) 4.624]. But in his proof of the existence of God Locke is not
supposing that our mental abilities show there is something
immaterial and spiritual about us. He does not use such a

thought in arguing that something immaterial must have produced us. His idea is rather that though matter might be arranged and be moved in such a way as to think, this could not happen by chance. Its doing so demands the prior existence of a thinking, purposeful being [*Ayres* 233 ff.]. Even if we are purely material beings we still require an immaterial cause.

The systematic science of ethics which Locke envisaged in the *Essay* caught the imagination of a friend, the Irish scientist, writer on astronomy and optics, William Molyneux (1656-98). More than once Molyneux pressed Locke actually to produce it and to oblige 'the World, with *a Treatise of Morals*, drawn up according to the Hints you frequently give in Your Essay, Of their Being Demonstrable according to the Mathematical Method' [*Locke* (6) 4.508]. Locke replied that he would, when he had the time, try to do something about it. '[Y]et whether I am able . . . is another question. Every one could not have demonstrated what Mr. Newton's book hath shewn to be demonstrable' [(6) 4.508]. He never did produce his demonstrative ethics but the failure to become the Newton of a science of morality and to produce an ethical *Principia* was of course not only his, as he points out elsewhere [(5) 7.140]. To admit that man's reason had failed to produce a complete and systematic body of ethical knowledge is not, however, to admit that it has failed completely in what Locke calls 'its great and proper business of morality' [(5) 7.140]. It is quite clear both from the *Essay* [I.iii.1,4, II.xxviii.8] and from the *Reasonableness of Christianity* that Locke believes the use of our reason has helped us to the possession of some truths of morality. But clear as it is that human reason does have some success in this area it is also clear that this does not come easily. 'Experience shows, that the knowledge of morality, by mere natural light . . . makes but a slow progress' [(5) 7.140]. Though reason is capable of attaining moral knowledge many people are poorly endowed with it. Not everyone has the time or ability needed to reason about morality. The 'long and sometimes intricate deductions of reason' which are involved in discovering moral principles are such that 'the greatest part of mankind have neither the leisure to weigh, nor, for want of education and use, skill to judge of' [(5) 7.139].

We know, of course, that our awareness of rules of morality is not innate. We saw in section 3 that Locke argues against the existence of innate practical principles of morality. But that moral principles are neither innate nor easy to discover by the use of reason does not mean that we are often left in the dark on these matters. We do not have to guess what our duties and obligations are. We find them in the Bible. Locke explains to Molyneux that 'the Gospel contains so perfect a body of Ethicks, that reason may be excused from that enquiry' [(6) 5.595].

In the *Reasonableness of Christianity* Locke distinguishes between using reason to discover an ethical truth and using it to verify and authenticate an apparent truth found in the Bible. It is far easier to find justifying arguments and rationales for ethical truths already promulgated in the Gospels than to discover them for oneself from scratch. In both cases the upshot is the same. So long as our awareness and grasp of a truth rests upon and has the backing of reason then, however we found it, we now have knowledge of it. But despite the fact that justification is easier than discovery many people are still not capable of verifying the Gospel teaching. So even though we have the Bible to show us the way to the possession of moral knowledge '[t]he greatest part cannot know, and therefore they must believe' [(5) 7.146].

Locke's distinction between knowledge proper on the one hand and belief on the other is familiar to us from earlier sections. A further detail of it is that belief or opinion which is derived from revelation is called by the special name of 'faith'. 'Faith . . . is the Assent to any Proposition, not . . . made out by the Deductions of Reason; but upon the Credit of the Proposer, as coming from GOD . . . . This way of discovering Truths to Men we call *Revelation*' [IV.xviii.2]. Locke devotes a whole chapter to the relation and interplay between knowledge and reason on the one hand, and faith, belief, and revelation on the other. Its general point is the supremacy of reason over revelation. This should be no surprise since from reason we get knowledge, from revelation mere 'belief' or 'opinion'. But the point is not simply that the productions of reason are superior to those of revelation. It is also that revelation is answerable to reason. Their respective realms are not completely separate. In principle there is the possibility that reason and what seems to be revelation might speak with conflicting voices.

It is already clear from what has been said about morality that 'the same Truths may be discovered, and conveyed down from Revelation, which are discoverable to us by Reason' [IV.xviii.4]. Reason could not verify what was found in the Bible were this not so. His view of these cases is that since any truth discovered by reason would be intuitively or demonstratively known it could not get any verification from revelation. Revelation could not make us any more certain of it. What is based on reason is more certain than what is based on revelation. For if we are to accept something on the basis of revelation we need to be certain that it is a genuine revelation. But we cannot be as certain of this as we are of our reason-based knowledge of the particular truth in question. 'The Knowledge, we have, that this Revelation came at first from GOD can never be so sure, as the Knowledge we have from the clear and distinct Perception of the Agreement, or Disagreement of our own Ideas' [IV.xviii.4].

Since the certainty of reason is greater than that of revelation because we can have no certainty that it *is* a revelation we obviously cannot accept on the basis of revelation anything *contrary* to reason. It would 'be to subvert the Principles, and Foundations of all Knowledge . . . [if] what we certainly know, give way to what we may possibly be mistaken in' [IV.xviii.5].

But though some moral truths might be reached both by reason and by revelation there are, we know already, limits to knowledge, and hence truths inaccessible to reason. Truths about the properties and powers of material substances, for example, are things of which 'by the natural Use of our Faculties, we can have no Knowledge at all' [IV.xviii.7]. Truths of this sort are, in Locke's phrase 'above Reason'. And they are, when revealed, 'purely Matters of *Faith*; with which *Reason* has, directly, nothing to do' [IV.xviii.7]. But of course not everything which is 'above Reason' has been the subject of a revelation. We would not expect it to be. We would not expect the beliefs of the natural philosopher for which he lacks the guarantee of reason, to be supported by revelation. But some things which are 'beyond the Discovery of our natural Faculties' have been revealed. Two examples are 'that part of the Angels rebelled against GOD' and 'that the dead shall rise, and live again' [IV.xviii.7].

The possibility of the revelation of things 'above Reason' is not an exception to Locke's general point that reason is superior to revelation. His precise words are that reason has 'directly, nothing to do' with such things. This leaves room for it to have something *indirectly* to do with them. Reason can say nothing about the truth or falsity of what is revealed in such cases. But it can say something about whether what we are confronted with is a genuine revelation. If something is a revelation from God it is, says Locke, bound to be true. 'But whether it be a divine Revelation, or no, *Reason* must judge' [IV.xviii.10]. Reason can say something also about the meaning or interpretation of the words in which the revelation is couched. What the Bible actually means may not be clear [III.ix.23].

There is a further way in which the Bible's revelation of things 'above Reason' does not involve a restriction on reason's supremacy. It is that acceptance of them is not necessary for salvation. The availability of and exposure to Holy Writ is not essential for the good of one's soul. Salvation is open to all simply by the use of our natural faculties. God, has 'given all Mankind so sufficient a light of Reason, that they to whom this written Word [the Bible] never came, could not (when-ever they set themselves to search) either doubt the Being of a GOD, or of the Obedience due to Him' [III.ix.23]. Locke's view that nothing necessary for salvation is 'above Reason' fits uneasily with his other view about the practical difficulty of rationally working our way to moral principles. It is all very well to say that everything necessary can in principle be worked out independently of the Bible. But if slow-minded and busy readers of the Bible can be thankful that it 'contains so perfect a body of Ethics that reason may be excused from that Enquiry' the position of those to whom it is unavailable is less happy than at first appeared.

According to Locke, then, beliefs based on revelation, items of faith, are to be regulated, whether directly or indirectly, by reason. This regulation by reason distinguishes faith from what

Locke, in the terminology of the time, calls 'enthusiasm'. A religious enthusiast is one who 'laying by Reason would set up Revelation without it' [IV.xix.3]. Locke speaks at length and with passion against enthusiasm. To accept a supposed revelation without using reason to decide its authenticity is to accept 'ungrounded Fancies' [IV.xix.3] or 'the Conceits of a warmed or over-weening Brain' [IV.xix.7]. An enthusiast will insist that reason should have nothing to do with revelation and faith, and claim that we are more open to inspiration if we put reason aside. Divine inspiration and revelation cannot, as an enthusiast supposes, be its own guarantee. The question must always be pressed 'How do I know that GOD is the Revealer of this to me; that this Impression is made upon my Mind by his holy Spirit, and that therefore I ought to obey it? If I know not this, how great soever the Assurance is that I am possess'd with, it is groundless; whatever Light I pretend to, it is but *Enthusiasm*' [IV.xix.10].

Locke's beliefs that reason has a central place in matters of religion and morality, and that it can discover the essentials for salvation place him in a broad stream of thought which flows at least from the time of the Restoration of Charles I on into the eighteenth century. During the Civil War and Cromwell's Commonwealth there had been a tendency in religion towards fanaticism and the extremes of 'enthusiasm'. Calvinism, which had been the official theology of the Commonwealth, encouraged a militant religiosity. Stress was laid on personal revelation and what was, in effect, arbitrary, idiosyncratic inspiration. The supernatural and mysterious aspects of religion were emphasised. Glanvill reports in 1670 how enthusiasm had brought '*Reason* into disgrace' and denied its use in religious matters. '[I]t hath brought into the world all kinds of *Phantastry* and *folly*, and exposed Religion to contempt and derision, by making *madness*, and *diseases sacred* ' [(2) 65]. With the Restoration in 1660 there came a reaction (evident in Glanvill's words) against the dogmatic pretences and intolerances of this emotional fanaticism. Moderation and reasonableness began to come to the fore. Sprat in 1667 refers to 'the late extravagent excesses of *Enthusiasm*. The infinite pretences to *Inspiration*, and· *immediat Communion* with God'. He is clearly relieved that 'the fierceness of *violent Inspirations* is in good measure departed' and that 'The universal Disposition of this *Age* is bent upon a *rational Religion*' [374-6].

The movements of Cambridge Platonism (involving such people as Henry More, Benjamin Whichcote, and Ralph Cudworth), and of Latitudinarianism (which involved many members of the Royal Society such as Sprat and Glanvill) encouraged the idea that solely by the use of his reason man could discern the essentials of religious belief and the means to salvation.[2] Perhaps relevation could supplement the discoveries of reason but it was not essential. This stress on what was called 'natural religion', discoverable by reason, did not at first necessarily mean the abandonment of Christianity as revealed in the Scriptures. We have seen that Locke held that so long as this was not inconsistent with reason it could be accepted. But towards the end of the century and into the next there began to emerge the deistic ideal that not merely the essentials but also the whole of religion could be discovered by reason, and that nothing should be a part of religion unless it was discoverable by reason. Locke certainly did much to foster rationalistic religion, but it must not be forgotten that he did not go this far.

We can now finally summarise Locke's conclusions about the 'extent of knowledge'. An important area which lies outside the bounds of human knowledge is natural philosophy, the field of study of his friends and colleagues in the recently formed Royal Society. There is a number of very basic questions in this area for which Locke thinks we can find no answer. How does the body act on the mind? How do bodies act on each other? So far these have been merely noted (in section 9) and have yet to be discussed in detail (in section 17). There are other less fundamental but equally important matters in natural philosophy about which we must remain ignorant. As we have seen in detail, we are ignorant of the real essences of material substances and so cannot have certain knowledge of their properties and powers. Natural philosophy is not a 'science' and is merely a body of 'opinion', 'belief', or, as might now be said, *a posteriori* knowledge. In this respect it is different from mathematics and geometry. Locke believes that in these areas we can have knowledge and construct a systematic body of demonstrative science. In this respect natural philosophy is different from morality too. Locke suggests that because we know the real essences of moral ideas a demonstrative science of ethical knowledge is possible. As yet, however, there has been no Euclid of moral science and so far our moral knowledge does not extend as far as it might. Indeed, due to the limitations of time or of intelligence not everyone can reason their way to any moral knowledge at all. Fortunately this does not matter so long as the Gospel is available. It must be remembered, though, that moral principles which are accepted not on the basis of reason and thought do not constitute knowledge. They amount merely to belief. The possbilities for human knowledge extend beyond mathematics, geometry, and ethics. We can have demonstrative knowledge of our own existence and of God. Moreover, just as we can *know* that God exists so we *know* we should obey his will. The essentials of salvation can be worked out by human reason and need not be matters of mere belief or faith.

Locke's definition of knowledge as perception of the agreement or disagreement between ideas was outlined in section 7. In effect three of the four sorts of agreement or disagreement he recognised have been dealt with. Locke's trifling propositions, discussed earlier in this section have to do with 'identity'; propositions in mathematics and geometry with 'relation'; and propositions about material substances with 'co-existence or necessary connexion'. The fourth sort of agreement was 'real existence'. It was noted in section 7 that it is not clear how the knowledge that God exists has to do with an agreement between ideas rather than between an idea and a thing. But beyond this, 'real existence' has not been much discussed. How far does knowledge of it extend? Locke answers this question in IV.xi and ii. 14-15. We have already seen that it extends as far as to encompass intuitive knowledge of our own existence and demonstrative knowledge of God's. But what about 'the particular existence of finite Beings without us' [IV.ii.14]? Do we really know that the material substances, the objects of the natural philosopher's observation and experiment, really exist? Locke thinks we do. '[T]he actual receiving of Ideas from without . . . gives us notice of the Existence of other Things, and makes us know, that something doth exist at that time without us, which causes that Idea in us' [IV.xi.2]. But is this really knowledge? Can we, strictly speaking, claim to know, on the basis of our having sensations and ideas, that something outside us causes those ideas? On the one hand Locke concedes, as clearly he has to, that it can be neither intuitive nor demonstrative knowledge. But on the other hand he is quite impatient with the suggestions of 'some Men' that an idea may be produced in their minds when no such object 'affects their Senses' [IV.ii.14], and that 'a Dream may do the same thing, and all these Ideas may be produced in us, without any external Objects' [IV.ii.14]. His way through is to say that though not absolute or perfect the certainty we can have here is so great that it 'deserves the name of Knowledge' [IV.xi.3] and 'passes under the name of Knowledge' [IV.ii.14]. He creates for it a new category, that of 'sensitive knowledge', alongside the two of demonstrative and intuitive knowledge. Locke's reference to 'some Men' who are 'so sceptical, as to maintain, that what I call being actually in the Fire, is nothing but a Dream; and that we cannot thereby certainly know, that any such thing as Fire actually exists without us' [IV.ii.14] could be to people impressed by Descartes' sceptical arguments in the first of his *Meditations*. Certainly it is because of Descartes that over the years much philosophical thought has been devoted to these questions. But Locke is not much interested in them. His category of sensitive knowledge is not so much a considered answer to them as a brusque shutting of the door on them.

In section 2 it was suggested that Locke's aim in the *Essay* of tracing how and to what extent we have knowledge, originated in specific questions about how the principles of morality are discovered and known to be true, and about what role revelation has as a source and foundation of morality and religion. We can see now that these specific questions were not simply forgotten and left behind but were answered along with others. It was also explained in section 2 that Locke might be placed in a tradition of constructive scepticism. As such his scepticism of course consists in the view, traced in some detail in the foregoing sections, that there are things we cannot know. Its constructive nature consists in the view that for our purposes and needs the knowledge we have is sufficient. It is an important and striking feature of Locke's attitude towards the human epistemological situation that he does not regret our inability to have certain knowledge in natural philosophy. It is not that he attaches no importance to and wishes to play down the practical benefits of acquaintance with the 'Powers, and Operations' [IV.iii.17] of material substances. He talks movingly of the difference that ignorance about how to smelt iron and what it might be used for could make to a whole civilization. '[T]o any one, that will seriously reflect on it, I suppose, it will appear past doubt, that were the use of Iron lost among us, we should in a few Ages be unavoidably reduced to the Wants and Ignorance of the ancient savage Americans, whose natural Endowments and Provisions come no way short of those of the most flourishing and polite Nations' [IV.xii.11]. Locke certainly does not underestimate the practical value of the endeavours of his colleagues in the Royal Society. On the contrary, it is precisely because these benefits have *already* been gained that our lack of demonstrative certainty in these matters should be of no concern or cause for regret. The *a posteriori* knowledge that we can gain on the basis of experience is quite sufficient to provide the means for a physically tolerable life. From 'Experiments and Historical Observations . . . we may draw Advantages of Ease and Health, and thereby increase our stock of Conveniences for this Life' [IV.xii.10]. Why regret that natural philosophy is not a science? There is no *practical* need for it to be so. It would, Locke thinks, be improper and unseemly meddling on our part to search after knowledge of substantial real essences and to want certain and demonstrative knowledge in natural philosophy. In his Journals he says of speculations of this sort that they are 'of noe solid advantage to us nor help to make our lives the happyer, they being but the uselesse imployment of idle or over curious brains which amuse them selves about things out of which they can by no means draw any reall benefit' [(7) 85].

The fact is that we 'have Cause enough to magnify the bountiful Author of our Being, for that Portion and Degree of Knowledge, he has bestowed on us'. He has given us 'Whatsoever is necessary for the Conveniences of Life' [I.i.5]. He has also given us the means to prove to ourselves that he exists and to ascertain what our duties and obligations are to him and our fellows. He has given us the means to discover the way to salvation. It is matters of this sort that are our proper concern. 'How short soever . . . [men's] Knowledge may come of an universal, or perfect Comprehension of whatsoever is, it yet secures their great Concernments, that they have Light enough to lead them to the Knowledge of their Maker, and the sight of their own Duties' [I.i.5; also 6]. It is of no practical importance that natural philosophy is not capable of being made a science. Demonstrative knowledge of material substances should be of no interest to us. We should rather spend our time on less theoretical concerns. 'Our proper Imployment lies in those Enquiries, and in that sort of Knowledge, which is most suited to our natural Capacities, and carries in it our greatest interest, *i.e.* the condition of our eternal Estate. Hence I think I may conclude, that *Morality* is *the proper Science, and Business of Mankind in general*' [IV.xii.11; also (7) 84 ff.].

Notes

1 *Aaron* 242; W. von Leyden, 'Locke and Nicole: Their Proofs of the Existence of God', *Sophia*, (1948).
2 Henry More (1614-87) was a philosopher and poet. Benjamin Whichcote (1609-83), teacher and preacher rather than writer, held that reason was 'the candle of the Lord'.

CHAPTER 4

16 'Some farther Considerations concerning our simple Ideas'

The *Essay's* aim is to enquire 'into the Original, Certainty, and Extent of humane Knowledge' [I.i.2]. We have been tracing that enquiry, and the last section has explained its findings. But certain details which were not crucial for understanding its general shape have so far been omitted. This and the next section will deal with some of them. This section is in effect concerned with a further detail of Locke's corpuscularianism and its bearing on Scholasticism.

In Book II Locke discusses 'Ideas'. We have already examined much of it. We have seen, for example, that ideas originate in experience and that they are to be divided into the simple and the complex. Chapter viii of Book II consists of 'Some farther Considerations concerning our simple Ideas'. In terms of the amount of comment and discussion it has provoked this relatively short and self-contained chapter is one of the more influential of the *Essay*. It falls into two parts. The first six paragraphs concern 'positive ideas and privative causes', and the remaining seventeen 'primary and secondary qualities'. According to its title it is about *ideas*, but this is misleading. It is about the physical production of ideas rather than ideas themselves. This concern with the causation of ideas makes the chapter into a 'little Excursion into Natural Philosophy' as Locke says at the end of it when he apologises for having been thus 'engaged in Physical Enquiries' [II.viii.22]. We should not imagine we have understood it properly, therefore, unless we have placed it against the background of the natural science of the time.

Locke begins with the obvious thought that all ideas of sensation, for example those of heat and cold, light and darkness, whiteness and blackness, are in some way or other caused or produced in the mind by the physical world acting on our senses. All these ideas are, as he says, 'equally clear and positive Ideas in the Mind' [II.viii.2]. Nevertheless perhaps only some of them are caused in a simple direct way by actually present causes. Perhaps others are caused by a lack or absence of these same causes. For example, 'the Idea of Black is no less positive . . . than that of White, however the cause of that Colour in the external Object, may be only a privation' [II.viii.3]. So though all *ideas* are positive, only some of them, Locke suggests, have *positive causes*. Others have negative or *privative causes*. Locke stresses that having a cause which is negative or privative does not mean that an idea is any the less positive. There is, he points out, a difference between words such as 'cold' or 'dark' which stand for positive ideas with privative causes, and negative words such as 'silence' or 'insipid' which stand for the absence of a positive idea [II.viii.5]. There is a difference between, as it were, an idea with an absent cause and the absence of an idea.

What Locke says about privation, an idea which goes back to Aristotle, is related to contemporary discussions. He expresses uncertainty at one point about the correctness of his examples of 'the privative causes I have here assigned of positive Ideas'. Nevertheless they are, he says, examples, 'according to the common Opinion' [II.viii.6]. The corpuscularian philosophers Epicurus and Gassendi would not have agreed with Locke's examples. They thought that cold was a positive quality. Nevertheless this 'common Opinion' is that associated with corpuscularianism and the new mechanical philosophy. It is certainly against this background that, in agreement with Locke's examples, Hobbes holds that black is a privation of light [1.464], and Descartes that cold is a privation of heat[(1) 1.164, 2.106]. The 'common Opinion' is also to be found, discussed in some detail, in Boyle's dialogue *Of the Positive and Privative Nature of Cold* and his essay *Of the Mechanical Origin of Heat and Cold* [see particularly 4.244]. Striking similarities can be found between Locke and Boyle on various aspects of this topic. The historical detail of the actual connexion is not clear.

But it should at any rate be noted that 1671 is the date of Locke's first mention of these matters, in draft B of the *Essay*, while 1674 and 1675 are the dates of publication of Boyle's two works.

The characters in Boyle's dialogue discuss the question whether cold, the cause of a certain idea in our minds, is 'a positive quality, or a bare privation of heat' [3.734]. They mention Cardan, [1] Descartes, and Descartes' followers, as holding, as Locke is tempted to, that cold is a privation. Aristotle and Gassendi are mentioned as holding otherwise.

Boyle discusses Gassendi at length. The arguments from his *Physicam* which aim to show that cold is not merely the absence of heat and that our idea of it is not produced by a privative cause are each carefully examined. One of them appeals to the undoubted fact that 'cold affects the organs of feeling, and sometimes causes great pain' [3.737]. It suggests that being an 'object of sense' in this way is incompatible with being a privation. As a consequence Gassendi was led to postulate corpuscles of cold. Through the mouth of the dialogue character Carneades, Boyle seeks to explain in reply that in corpuscularian terms there is no contradiction in a positive idea having a privative cause [3.737-8, 743]. As we know, Boyle's theory does not attribute non-mechanical properties like heat (leave alone cold) to the particles themselves. What he says as a preliminary to his account of the production of the idea of cold is identical with Locke's explanation of 'why a privative cause might, in some cases at least, produce a positive Idea':

> Sensation being produced in us, only by different degrees and modes of Motion in our animal Spirits, variously agitated by external Objects, the abatement of any former motion, must as necessarily produce a new sensation, as the variation or increase of it; and so introduce a new Idea, which depends only on a different motion of the animal Spirits in that Organ. [II.viii.4]

Locke's explanation did not satisfy Lee. Since 'Every *Abatement* . . . of the *Degree* of Motion, or *Alteration* of its kind, is *another* sort of Motion', what Locke says involves, Lee felt, only different positive causes and not, as was intended, positive and privative causes [54]. So far as merely different degrees of motion are concerned Lee obviously has a point. Locke's kind of explanation would be most successful in cases which involved the difference between ideas following on from moving animal spirits and ideas following on from stationary spirits. But Locke too is not entirely happy with the explanation, and expresses doubt about it even in such cases. He concludes his whole discussion by admitting that 'in truth it will be hard to determine, whether there be really any Ideas from a privative cause, till it be determined, Whether Rest be any more a privation than Motion' [II.viii.6].

The parallel between Boyle and Locke goes beyond Boyle's preliminary to his account of the idea of cold. It extends also to the account itself [3.735-6, 737-8, 743] which is identical with what Locke says at II.viii.21. There are further striking similarities in their use of the example of shadows and light [II.viii.5/ 3.738]. Moreover Locke's explanation of how an appearance of black can, unlike the appearance of white, have a privative cause [II.viii.2] is in effect a brief summary of Boyle's [1.704 f.].

In dealing with privative causes Locke was clearly taking part in a contemporary discussion. What he says passes almost unnoticed now, and the vast amount of comment this chapter has provoked is focussed entirely on the second of its two topics, that of primary and secondary qualities. In moving on to this Locke carefully distinguishes between the *qualities* of objects and the perceptions and sensations, the *ideas*, which those qualities produce in our minds. He thus makes quite clear that the primary/secondary distinction which he goes on to draw is not one between kinds of ideas in the mind. It is between kinds of quality in objects.

Primary or *original* qualities are 'such as are utterly inseparable from the Body . . . in all the alterations . . . it suffers' [II.viii.9]. Locke explains what he means by the inseparability of primary qualities from parts of matter by saying that the parts of a grain of wheat even if they are further subdivided are each always still solid, extended, of a certain shape, and potentially if not actually in motion. At one point or another he gives as primary qualities solidity, extension, figure, mobility (motion or rest), and number. These, it should be noted, are no more and no less than the qualities which Boyle's corpuscular hypothesis attributes to the insensible particles of matter.

Secondary qualities are 'such Qualities, which in truth are nothing in the Objects themselves, but Powers to produce various Sensations in us by their primary Qualities, *i.e.* by the Bulk, Figure, Texture, and Motion of their insensible parts, as Colours, Sounds, Tasts, *etc.*' [II.viii.10]. It may seem from this that Locke intends *texture* as a primary quality. But what he means by 'texture' is what Boyle meant by it. Boyle, as we saw in section 12, says that 'when many corpuscles do . . . convene together as to compose any distinct body . . . then from their [size and shape] . . . there doth emerge a certain disposition or contrivance of parts in the whole, which we may call the texture of it' [3.22]. Texture is not a primary quality, which corpuscles can have by themselves. It is a property of a *collection* of corpuscles which results from the primary qualities of the corpuscles in the collection and from the way in which they are arranged and spatially related to each other. Locke is not intending texture as a further primary quality which the insensible parts of matter may have. He is simply saying, along with Boyle, that colours and tastes of objects depend not only on the primary qualities of their insensible parts but also on the resulting texture of the parts taken together.

Against the background of this distinction between primary and secondary qualities Locke goes on to give a physical explanation of perception. 'Bodies produce Ideas in us', he says, 'by impulse' [II.viii.11]. This is 'the only way which we can conceive Bodies operate in'. So unless objects are actually 'united to our minds' the last stage of perception must be the transfer of motion from our sense-organs, through our bodies, 'to the Brains or the seat of Sensation, there to produce in our Minds . . . particular Ideas' [II.viii.12]. This motion in our sense-organs is initiated by 'singly imperceptible Bodies' coming from the sensed objects. Some passages give the impression that these corpuscles which travel between a sensible object and our sense-organs are emitted by the object. If they are, then one may wonder how 'to explain the apparently inexhaustible supply of corpuscles that bodies have and can send out' [*Yolton* (2) 37]. Of course things do lose their smell and taste but not their 'looks', as it were. It may be, however, that the 'singly imperceptible Bodies' moving between observed and observer are the particles of light to which Locke refers elsewhere [IV.iii.15; also II.viii.19].

Though Locke is actually not explicit about this, the insensible material corpuscles do not themselves have colour, taste, or any other secondary quality. Since an object's colour results from the primary qualities of its component particles and their consequent texture, single corpuscles can have no colour. But though imperceptible corpuscles have only primary qualities, primary qualities are not had only by imperceptible corpuscles. As well as having the various secondary qualities, perceptible large-scale objects also have the primary qualities of size, shape, and the rest.

From what he has said so far about primary and secondary qualities Locke draws a corollary about resemblance between ideas and qualities. He seems to think the point is quite obvious but it is something on which much discussion has focussed. The ideas of the primary qualities of bodies are 'Resemblances of them, and their Patterns do really exist in the Bodies themselves'. But the ideas produced by secondary qualities 'have no resemblance of them at all':

> There is nothing like our Ideas, existing in the Bodies themselves. They are in the Bodies, we denominate from them, only a Power to produce those Sensations in us: And what is Sweet, Blue, or Warm in Idea, is but the certain Bulk, Figure, and Motion of the insensible Parts in the Bodies themselves. [II.viii.15]

How are some ideas 'resemblances' of qualities in bodies, and some not [II.viii.7, 16, 18]? What does Locke mean that some qualities are 'real' and 'really exist in . . . Bodies' whereas others are 'nothing in the Objects themselves, but Powers to produce various Sensations in us' even though 'by mistake' we attribute 'reality' to them [II.viii.14, 15, 17, 18, 24]?

One popular interpretation has it that Locke has in mind facts about perceptual error and illusion. We can make mistakes about the properties of things which often appear to be other than what they really are. Thus one commentator says that the only way to understand Locke's claim of 'resemblance' between our ideas and primary qualities but not between them and secondary qualities is to take him to mean that whereas we do not fall into perceptual error about, say, the shape of things we do about, say, their colour [*Aaron* 126]. Another supposes similarly that Locke is saying that our perception of colour as opposed to that of shape varies 'with the position of the observer and with his physical and mental state' [*O'Connor* 65]. Of course Locke would be wrong about this for we can be mistaken about shape, and apparent shape is sometimes relative to the observer. It is felt, nevertheless, that this is the sort of thing he has in mind.

Recently this interpretation has been increasingly opposed. It is becoming accepted that what Locke says about 'resemblance' has nothing to do with perceptual error and needs to be set more firmly than previously in the context of corpuscularianism. Against this background it has been said that the claim that ideas of primary qualities have 'resemblances' in objects records the fact that primary qualities enter into the corpuscularian explanation of the causation of ideas of shape, size, and so on.[2] The corresponding claim that ideas of secondary qualities do not have 'resemblances' means that no reference to such qualities (but, again, only to primary qualities) is made in the explanation of the production of ideas of colour, taste, and so on. The shape of an object and the shapes of insensible corpuscles are both elements in the production of the idea of shape. The colour of an object, however, is nothing but a power to produce certain ideas in us – a power which is a function of, again, the primary qualities of insensible particles. This suggestion about what Locke's talk of 'resemblance' means is worth exploring further.

As I have said, Locke thinks it an obvious corollary of his distinction between primary and secondary qualities that ideas of the ones do and ideas of the others do not have 'resemblances' in objects. But he does not think that in and by itself this claim will be obvious to everybody. On the contrary he says that there is 'commonly thought' to be a 'perfect resemblance' as 'in a mirror' between the whiteness of snow and of manna and our idea of it. It would 'by most Men be judged very extravagent, if one should say otherwise' [II.viii.16]. Why is it that we make this mistake and 'are so forward to imagine, that those Ideas [of secondary qualities] are the resemblances of something really existing in the Objects themselves'? It is, says Locke, because there is nothing about ideas of secondary qualities which makes it obvious that they can be explained by reference to primary qualities alone [II.viii.25]. Given this reason one might naturally suppose that the common mistake which Locke takes himself to be correcting is one made by the man in the street. One might naturally take it to be a mistake which might be as easily made today as in the seventeenth century. Locke's references to what 'Men' think and to what is 'generally' or 'usually' thought certainly do not contradict this [II.viii.2, 7,18]. But we need to appreciate that what he is rejecting is not simply a vulgar or common error. It is also part of Scholastic theory. It is a pity that though what Locke says on this topic is increasingly being seen to be connected with his corpuscularianism, its elements of anti-Scholasticism are barely acknowledged.

Just as the corpuscularian theory of matter did not begin with Locke so the primary/secondary quality distinction, or something like it, can be found in earlier atomists such as Democritus and Galileo. As we might expect, it can be found in Boyle too. In the light of what he says we will be able to see more clearly what the anti-Scholastic features of Locke's discussion are. He refers, in the *Origin of Forms*, to a 'grand mistake that hath hitherto obtained about the nature of qualities' [3.18]. This grand mistake is that of supposing that 'whiteness . . . is a real entity which denominates the parcel of matter to which it is joined, white' [3.13]. It is that of supposing that qualities are 'real and distinct entities', of supposing that fire has an 'inherent quality of heat' and of supposing that 'sensible qualities are real beings in the objects they denominate' [3.17,23,26]. Boyle completely rejects this view that 'real qualities [are not] . . . either matter or modes of matter' and have 'a nature distinct from the modification of the matter they belong to' [3.12,17]. He urges against it that 'there is in the body, to which these sensible qualities are attributed, nothing of the real and physical but the size, shape, and motion or rest, of its component particles, . . . nor is it necessary that they should have in them any thing more, like to the ideas they occasion in us'

[3.23]. All of this has echoes in the *Essay*, of course. Locke too speaks of the mistake of supposing that there is something like our ideas of colour 'in objects'. He too refers to the error of taking certain qualities to be 'real' and to 'really exist in bodies'.

Locke gave some indication that the mistake was one made by the ordinary person. Boyle similarly speaks as though it is to be attributed simply to the man in the street. He says that 'we have been from our infancy apt to imagine that these sensible qualities are real beings in the objects they denominate, and have the faculty or power to work such and such things' [3.23]. He says that certain of our perceptions 'are commonly imagined to proceed from certain distinct and peculiar qualities in the external objects which have some resemblance to the ideas their action upon the senses excites in the mind' [3.36]. But he makes plain also that these mistaken ideas, or at any rate some formal or technical expression of them, form a part of Scholastic theory. It is, he says, 'the schools [who] have of late much amused the world with [their talk of] . . . real qualities . . . [to which they] attribute . . . a nature distinct from the modification of the matter they belong to' [3.12]. It is the schools who 'if . . . it be demanded how snow comes to dazzle the eyes, . . . will answer, that it is by a quality of whiteness that is in it which makes all very white bodies produce the same effect'. It is the schools who 'if you ask what this whiteness is . . . will tell you . . . that it is a real entity which denominates the parcel of matter to which it is joined, white' [3.12-13]. It is 'scholastick opinion touching real qualities and accidents . . . [that] will not allow these accidents to be modes of matter, but entities really distinct from it' [3.17]. So what Boyle characterises and attacks as the 'grand mistake' of supposing that 'sensible qualities are real beings in the objects they denominate' and 'have some resemblance to the ideas their action upon the senses excites in the mind' should not be seen simply as a vulgar or common error. It is also embodied in Scholastic theory. Norris is quite explicit that the 'grand mistake' is simultaneously an error of the man in the street and a piece of Scholastic sophistication. A few years later than the *Essay* he comments that 'none of those sensible Qualities which the Philosophy of the School, as well as the Imagination of the Vulgar is pleased to attribute to Bodies

... have any real existence in Bodies' [2.250]. Years earlier Hobbes had begun to explain how a common unthinking error could come to have a technical expression in a Scholastic theory. He remarked that while it is 'no hard matter' for someone to suppose that his perceptions of qualities 'are the *very qualities themselves*' a whole Scholastic apparatus 'is necessary for the maintenance of that opinion' [4.4].

These quotations make obvious just which element of Scholasticism is in question here. One thing Boyle evidently has in mind is the practice, described in section 12, of explaining by citing at the explanatory level something entirely analogous to what is to be explained. He is again complaining about the attempt to explain the whiteness of snow, by appeal to 'a real entity which denominates the parcel of matter to which it is joined, white' [3.13]. He is rejecting the supposition that colour is 'an inherent quality of the object in the sense that is wont to be declared by the schools' [1.671]. He is suggesting instead that 'there is in the body that is said to be coloured, a certain disposition of the superficial particles, whereby it sends the light reflected, or refracted, to our eyes thus and thus altered, and not otherwise' [1.671].

When we read Locke against this Boylean background it inevitably appears that he is rejecting just this same element of Scholasticism. He is rejecting it when he says that 'What is Sweet, Blue, or Warm in Idea, is but the certain Bulk, Figure and Motion, of the insensible Parts in the Bodies themselves, which we call so' [II.viii.15]. His suggestion that secondary qualities are nothing inherent in the object is a rejection of the forms and real qualities of the Scholastics.

But though Boyle and Locke are attacking the real qualities of what they see as the easy, contentless explanations of the Scholastics there is more to it than this. The anti-Scholastic bent of their remarks about primary and secondary qualities in effect consists of two separable strands. First there is one to the effect that secondary qualities are nothing but powers which bodies have by virtue of the primary qualities of their insensible parts. According to this, secondary qualities are nothing inherent in objects. They are not 'real qualities' which have 'a nature distinct from the modifications of the matter they belong to'. This strand has been explained in the previous paragraph in terms of a rejection of the Scholastic approach to explanation. But there is a second strand which runs through Locke's and Boyle's remarks. It shows itself in Locke's case in the claims that our ideas of secondary qualities are not the 'likeness of something existing without us', and that the ideas produced in us by these secondary qualities 'have no resemblance of them at all' [II.viii.7,15]. It comes out in Boyle's case in his denial that the perceptions in our minds of heat and colour 'proceed from certain distinct and peculiar qualities in the external objects which have some resemblance to the ideas their action upon the senses excites in the mind'. Though both of these strands are present in both Locke and Boyle the first is the more marked in Boyle, and the second in Locke. Boyle's anti-Scholasticism tends to show itself in the simple claim that certain qualities are not 'real and distinct entities' but are modifications of matter. Locke's usually shows itself in the insistence that there is no resemblance between those qualities and our ideas of them.

What exactly is this second line of thought which runs through Locke's and Boyle's remarks? The first, as I have explained, concerns the rejection of Scholastic explanations of the observable qualities and properties of things and their replacement by corpuscular explanations. But we need an explanation of more than objects having the various properties they do have. We might also seek to explain the phenomenon of our perception of these properties. Just as we might ask, 'Why is this thing white, that thing red?', so we might also ask what is going on when we perceive these colours. It is the phenomenon of our perception of the properties of things, as opposed to those properties themselves which is the concern of the second strand of Locke's and Boyle's thought. Locke's frequent, and Boyle's less frequent, remarks about the lack of resemblance between certain of our ideas and the qualities of which they are ideas need to be seen against the background of the Scholastic theory of sense-perception.

Modern discussions make plain that the Scholastics' account of perception was connected with their explanations of the properties of things.[3] Just as explanation was in terms of the substantial and accidental forms of the hylemorphic theory so the essential character of sensation was supposed to be the apprehension of form without matter. The senses were supposed to receive forms without matter as wax receives the impression of a ring without the metal. Thus seventeenth-century accounts speak of resemblances of the real qualities of objects being transmitted to the eye. Indeed Descartes went so far as to say that 'the principal reason' the Scholastics posited real qualities was 'that they thought that the perceptions of the senses could not be explained without assuming them' [2.250]. Malebranche, who went on to criticise the theory, described it in this way. 'The most commonly held opinion [about the production of ideas in the mind by material things] is that of the Peripatetics who hold that external objects transmit species that resemble them . . . . They call these species *impressed*, because objects impress them on the external senses [Bk.3, sect. 2, ch. 3; also *Norris* 2.333 ff.].

The Scholastic theory of sense-perception was often attacked in the seventeenth century. Some broadly corpuscularian or mechanical account was usually offered in its place. Hobbes suggested that sensation and perception is caused by 'the motion, of external things upon our eyes' through the 'mediation of the nerves, and other strings and membranes of the body'. 'But', he then says, 'the philosophy-schools . . . grounded upon certain texts of Aristotle, teach another doctrine'. They say 'for the cause of *vision*, that the thing seen, sendeth forth on every side a *visible species* . . . the receiving whereof into the eye, is *seeing*' [3.2-3]. Along similar lines Glanvill said that

> the diversity of our Sensations ariseth from the diversity of the *motion* or *figure* of the object; which in a different manner affect the Brain . . . . [Sensation results] from the so differing *configuration* and *agitation* of their *Particles*: and not from, I know not what *Chimerical beings*, supposed to inhere in the objects, their cause, and thence to be propagated by many petty *imaginary productions* to the seat of *Sense*. [(1) 88]

Boyle is alluding to the Scholastics' theory of sense-perception when, in describing their 'grand mistake', he refers to the supposition that our perceptions 'proceed from certain distinct and peculiar qualities in the external objects which have some resemblance to the ideas their action excites in the mind'. Locke also has it in mind when *he* denies there to be resemblance between certain of our ideas and the qualities of which they are ideas. Locke and Boyle clearly wish to replace this Scholastic theory of perception by their own corpuscularian account.

There is no direct evidence in the *Essay* that Locke's causal account of perception (and his consequent denial that many of our ideas have resemblances in objects) is an attack on the Scholastics. His solitary explicit reference to Peripatetic *species* is made only in passing [III.x.14]. But there is direct evidence in his *Examination of Malebranche* that his target is Scholasticism. We noted that Malebranche raises a number of difficulties for the Peripatetic account. Locke, in his examination of these pages, is anxious to point out that *he* does not hold that 'the resemblance of things' is carried by 'material species . . . from the body we perceive' [(5) 9.215]. He stresses that the difficulties there are in this view can be coped with perfectly well on his own account. What he proposes is, in effect, the mechanistic account we have already seen him putting forward in the *Essay*. So it is reasonable to suppose that he had the Peripatetic doctrine in mind in the *Essay* when, in putting forward his own view, he denied that our ideas of secondary qualities 'resemble' qualities 'really in the bodies' themselves.

Towards the end of chapter viii Locke discusses a number of examples of perception and sensation. He mentions that the colour of porphyry cannot be seen in the dark, that the colour and taste of an almond is altered when it is beaten up in a pestle and that the same water may 'produce the Sensation of Heat in one hand, and Cold in the other'. I referred earlier to a well-established interpretation according to which Locke's distinction between primary and secondary qualities has to do with the idea that we are often in perceptual error and subject to illusion about colours, tastes, and so on. According to this interpretation Locke's examples are intended to show that our perception of secondary qualities is often illusory. We have seen, however, that what really lies behind Locke's distinction is his preference for a corpuscularian as opposed to a Scholastic explanation of the properties of bodies, and, in particular, of our perception of them. Accordingly, his examples are to be seen as illustrations of how certain obvious facts can be made sense of and explained in terms of a corpuscularian theory of perception.

There is no need to suppose that Locke is showing that the changes in the colour and taste of an almond *must* be explained in corpuscular terms [*Bennett* 103]. He is doing no more than showing that they *can* be. Boyle, who goes into far greater factual detail on the matter and to whom Locke would surely have deferred, never claims more than this. In a work explicitly devoted to *The Mechanical Origin or Production of divers particular Qualities* he says:

> if I took upon me to demonstrate, that the qualities of bodies cannot proceed from (what the Schools call) substantial forms, or from any other causes but mechanical, it might be reasonably enough expected, that my argument should directly exclude them all. But . . . I pretend only, that they may be explicated by mechanical principles, without enquiring, whether they are explicable by any other. [4.232]

So, in an account of the origin of tastes and colours, Boyle argues that

> if, by bare mechanical change of the internal disposition and structure of a body, a permanent quality, confessed to flow from its substantial form . . . be abolished . . . such a phaenomenon will not a little favour that hypothesis, which teaches, that these qualities depend upon certain contextures, and other mechanical affections of the small parts of the bodies. [4.232]

The point of Locke's examples is not, as used commonly to be held, to show that we are prone to error in our perception of some qualities. It is to illustrate how certain perceptual facts can, however the Scholastics might have dealt with them, easily be made sense of in corpuscular terms. The porphyry example shows this very nicely. The colours of porphyry, as indeed of anything else, cannot be seen in the dark. But, asks Locke,

> Can any one think any real alterations are made in the Porphyre, by the presence or absence of Light; and that those Ideas of whiteness and redness, are really in Porphyre in the light, when 'tis plain it has no colour in the dark? . . . [W]hiteness or redness are not in it at any time, but such a texture, that hath the power to produce such a sensation in us. [II.viii.19]

The question whether there are colours in the dark was not Locke's own. It had been discussed in classical times and was again being discussed in the seventeenth century. Boyle refers to it as 'that famous controversy which was of old disputed betwixt the Epicureans and other Atomists on one side, and most other philosophers on the other' [1.690]. He says that the former denied 'bodies to be coloured in the dark' while the others asserted 'colour to be an inherent quality'. Telling us that the controversy had recently been revived and 'hotly agitated amongst the moderns' Boyle unsurprisingly aligns himself with the ancient atomists. He goes on to give a detailed account of the matter, an account of which what Locke says is a mere summary. When we remember Boyle's report that the Schools held colours to be 'inherent and real qualities, which the light doth but disclose' [1.693] it is clear which side of the argument they took. Norris makes this quite explicit. In answer to the question 'Are there colours in the dark?', he says, 'the Philosophers of the School will tell you that there are, tho' we do not see them' [2.248].

Like the porphyry example, Locke's example of the warm water feeling hot to one hand and cold to the other, is one which was discussed at the time, notably by Boyle. Examination of it would again show Locke aiming to illustrate how the corpuscular hypothesis can make good sense of a fact of perception which otherwise might appear to be (in Boyle's phrase) 'a paradox' [2.481].

Notes

[1] Jerome Cardan (1501-76) was an Italian mathematician, astrologer and physician. His *De Subtilitate Rerum* (1550) to which Boyle refers is a work of physical learning and speculation.

[2] E.M. Curley, 'Locke, Boyle, and the distinction between primary and secondary qualities', *Philosophical Review*, 81 (1972), pp. 451 ff.

[3] See M. Boas, 'Boyle as a theoretical scientist,' *Isis*, 41 (1950), p.262, and 'The Establishment of the Mechanical Philosophy', *Osiris*, 10 (1952), p.415; and M. Carré, *Realists and Nominalists* (Oxford Univeristy Press, London, 1946), pp. 81-100.

17 Body and Mind

In talking about the 'Extent' of Knowledge in IV.iii.28-9 Locke gives a number of cases where we are 'utterly uncapable of universal and certain Knowledge'. One type of case concerns the properties and powers of material substances. We have traced in detail his view that we can have no certain knowledge of these because of our ignorance of real essences. Other cases, as we noted in section 9, concerned certain basic facts about minds and bodies. How does body act on mind? How do bodies act on each other? The detail of these radical problems about body and mind will come out in this section. The context in which what Locke says about body and mind needs to be placed is formed partly by Descartes' very influential views about them and partly by the corpuscularianism of the time.

What is meant by 'body' here is not, as the *Pocket Oxford Dictionary* has it, 'a man or animal dead or alive'. Rather it is 'body' simply as 'piece of matter'. We have already seen, in sections 11,12, and 13, something of what Locke thinks about matter and material substance. But there is more to be said, in particular about the contrast between matter, and mind or spirit. The two are distinguished in a number of passages in Book II, chapter xxiii. Locke says that 'Body is a thing that is extended, figured, and capable of Motion; a Spirit a thing capable of thinking' [3; also 15, 17, 30]. Then, again, he says later that 'Our Idea of Body, as I think, is an extended solid Substance, capable of communicating Motion by impulse: and our Idea of our Soul, as an immaterial Spirit, is of a Substance that thinks, and has a power of exciting Motion in Body, by Will, or Thought' [22].

If we concentrate first on body or material substance we should note that, according to Locke, part of the essence of this is to be extended and solid. He was not alone in his belief that solidity is part of the essence of body. He shared it with others such as Boyle and Newton. But the belief was not universally held. A rival view was that solidity was not necessary to body and that extension alone was its whole essence. Locke acknowledges this when he mentions that 'There are some that would persuade us, that Body and Extension are the same thing' [II.xiii.11]. As he makes explicit elsewhere, he has in mind here Descartes and his followers [IV.vii.12, (1) 42-3, 78, 100]. In the *Principles* Descartes distinguished two kinds of created things or substances: soul or mind or spirit, and body. Each has 'one principle property . . . which constitutes its nature and essence' [(1) 1.240]. In the case of body this is extension: 'extension in length, breadth and depth, constitutes the nature of corporeal substance' [(1) 1.240]. Thus 'the nature of matter or of body . . . does not consist in its being hard, or heavy, or coloured . . . but solely in the fact that it is a substance extended in length, breadth and depth' [(1) 1.255-6]. Locke completely rejected Descartes' view about the identity of body and extension. He makes a number of points against it. Sadly, however, these tend to be little more than initial difficulties about which Descartes had already said something. Disingenuity about what he must have known Descartes had said is not the only thing of which Locke can be accused. He also makes the mistake, against which a recent writer has warned, of supposing that 'ordinary assumptions . . . about sensible objects should have any easy connection with the conceptual system of the *Principles*' [*Wilson* 87]. He writes as though Descartes' views are naive in the extreme and open to swift conclusive refutation.

His first objection is that extension by itself is insufficient to constitute body and so it cannot be identical with it. Body, he argues, has some property upon which 'depends its filling of Space, its Contact, Impulse, and Communication of Motion upon Impulse' [II.xiii.11]. This further property is, he suggests, solidity, or 'impenetrability' [II.iv.1], which is something which should be distinguished from hardness [II.iv.4 f.]. It is because of their solidity that bodies are able 'to fill space' [II.iv.2; also 5], and to enter into collision with and push or be pushed by each other [II.iv.2]. Before Locke, Leibniz had already objected to the Cartesian identification of body and

extension on exactly these same grounds. But his own positive
position is different from Locke's. It coincides with it in that
they both think that impenetrability is sufficient for the filling
of space. But whereas Locke thinks that 'Upon the Solidity of
Bodies also depends their mutual Impulse, Resistance, and
Protusion' [II.iv.5] Leibniz does not. The ability to enter into
collisions requires further properties [*Broad* 55].

Locke's next point against the idea that extension forms the
whole essence of body is that body and space are quite plainly
different [II.xiii.13-14]. Body can be divided into parts and the
parts moved away from each other. Space cannot. 'The Parts of
pure Space are inseparable one from the other' and 'immov-
able'. As it stands this objection completely ignores Descartes'
own serious and open recognition of these obvious differences.
Locke could hardly have been ignorant of Descartes' attempt to
show that the differences are more apparent than real, and that
space is different from body only 'in our mode of conceiving it'
[(1) 1.260]. He seems merely to be rehearsing a commonplace
initial objection and wilfully ignoring the answer which Descartes and the Cartesians had already provided.

Locke also suggests against the Cartesian identification that
surely space is unlimited while body is not:

> If Body be not supposed infinite, which, I think, no man will affirm, I
> would ask, Whether if God had placed a Man at the extremity of corporeal
> Beings, he could not stretch his Hand beyond his Body? . . . The Truth is,
> these Men must either own, that they think Body infinite, though they are
> loth to speak it out, or else affirm, that Space is not Body. [II.xiii.21]

It may seem simply untrue that the Cartesians are unwilling to
say that body is infinite. After all, as a consequence of his
identification of body and extension, Descartes admitted that
'this world, or the totality of corporeal substance, is extended
without limit' [(1) 1.264]. But in his correspondence with
Henry More, Descartes shows the reticence of which Locke
speaks. For reasons which do not matter here he insists on a
distinction between 'indefinite' and 'infinite', and despite much
urging will allow that space (and hence body) can only be said
to be indefinite, not infinite.

Locke's appeal to 'a Man at the extremity of corporeal

Being . . . stretch[ing] his Hand beyond his Body' into empty space is, as Lee remarked, an '*old* Argument' [74]. It goes back, in fact, to the fourth century B.C. Archytas of Tarentum used it in support of the Pythagorean belief in infinite empty space beyond the world and against the Cartesian-like belief of the Eliatic school that body and space coincide. As Lee again recognised, Locke's next argument is equally old. The Eliatic philosopher Parmenides believed that body and space were identical. He therefore held that motion is impossible since there would be nowhere for bodies to move into. Locke agrees that there is a connexion between motion and empty space. But he reverses the direction of Parmenides' argument. Believing that motion is possible he concludes that body and space are not identical [II.xiii.22]. The parallels between classical Greek and seventeenth-century European thought go further still. In the fifth century B.C. Empedocles rejected the idea that empty space is necessary for motion. So long as things simultaneously move into each others' places motion is possible in a plenum just as it is in a crowd. This was in fact the Cartesian answer to the kinds of objection raised by Locke. Motion is possible even though space and body are identical, for 'one body expels another from the place that it is entering, and this in turn expels another, and another, and so on until the last one to be moved moves into the place left by the first at the very moment that it becomes vacant' [(2) 356]. Again Locke raises the objection as though in complete ignorance of any possible Cartesian answer to it. But he would not ask, as he does elsewhere, whether 'one cannot have the idea of one body moved, while others are at rest' unless he were fully aware of the detail of the Cartesian position on local motion.

From his identification of space and body Descartes deduced, indeed he laid it down as a principle, that 'it is contrary to reason to say that there is a vacuum or space in which there is absolutely nothing' [(1) 1.262]. Locke avoids any mock-innocence on this point. He refrains from 'objecting' to the Cartesian identification that it rules out a vacuum. It was a too notorious and discussed fact for him to do this. Instead he tries to show that a vacuum is not inconceivable. He suggests, for one thing, that· a vacuum must be possible or else enquiries and disputes about the matter would be incoherent [II.xiii.23, iv.3]. Moreover, God surely could create a vacuum by keeping all matter in the universe at rest and annihilating one part of it. '[T]he Space, that was filled by the parts of the annihilated Body, will still remain, and be a Space without Body' [II.xiii.21, *bis*]. But though he is beginning at least to scratch the surface of the Cartesian view in trying to show that a vacuum is possible what he says is still disingenuously naive. His 'argument' is simply a version of what Descartes had openly raised as a 'prejudice concerning the absolute vacuum' [(1) 1.263]. Descartes had replied to the prejudice that 'if God removed all the body contained in a vessel without permitting its place being occupied by another body . . . the sides of the vessel will thereby come into immediate contiguity with one another' [(1) 1.263]. What Locke produces as an 'objection' is an intimate part of the very exposition of Descartes' views in the *Principles*. He could hardly have known of the doctrines without also knowing of the doctrinal answers to his 'objections'. Locke hardly engages properly and seriously with the important detail of Descartes' position.

We have already seen that for Locke bodies are extended because they are solid. It is because of their solidity that they 'fill space'. But Locke finds a problem in how the parts of solid body cohere to form an extended whole. The parts of a solid such as ice cohere in a way in which those of a liquid such as water or of sand in an hour-glass do not [II.xxiii.25, 26]. How do the 'solid parts of Body . . . [keep united], or cohere together to make Extension' [II.xxiii.23]? '[W]e shall', he says, 'very ill comprehend the extension of Body, without understanding wherein consists the union and cohesion of its parts' [II.xxiii.24].

This question of cohesion was first raised by the classical atomists Leucippus and Democritus. Consequently it was much discussed in the seventeenth century with the revival of atomism. Locke's final view is that cohesion is incomprehensible. He wrote to Stillingfleet in 1699 that matter 'has its parts connected by ways inconceivable to us' [(5) 4.466; also II.xxiii.26, IV.iii.29]. Earlier in the century More, too, had found that we 'cannot at all imagine' the cause of cohesion

[66,81], and Glanvill had remained sceptical about the possibility of explaining it [(1) 48 ff.]. At the time of the early drafts of the *Essay*, however, Locke appeared to think that in principle there was no particular difficulty. If we could but perceive the minute particles of water and ice 'we should as well know the very modus or way whereby cold produces hardnesse and consistency in water, as we doe the way how a joyner puts several peices of wood togeather to make a box or table which by tenants nails, and pins we well enough perceive how it is made to hang togeather' [(1) 30; also (2) 278]. Locke seems to be thinking here of the kind of explanation atomism had traditionally offered in terms of hooks, and spikes, and of entanglements of differently shaped atoms. It was an explanation which Gassendi[1] had offered and one which Boyle did not reject [4.307, 1.401]. But by the time Locke came to write the *Essay* he was obviously dissatisfied with it. Any appeal to any 'Bonds' or 'Cement' [II.xxiii.26] to explain cohesion simply puts the problem one step further back. Glanvill had been similarly dissatisfied. 'If it be pretended . . . that the parts of solid bodies are held together by *hooks*, and *angulous* involutions . . . the *coherence* of the parts of these *hooks* . . . will be of as difficult a conception, as the former' [(1) 50].

There were other explanations of cohesion. Boyle discusses a Scholastic account based on substantial forms [1.411]. Very influential, however, was the Cartesian theory according to which 'there is nothing that joins the parts of hard bodies excepting that they are in repose' [(1) 1.268]. This theory was one amongst the others that Boyle in his eclectic way accepted [1.402, 411]. Glanvill objected to it with robust common sense. '[I]f the *Union* of the *Parts* consist only in *Rest*; it would seem that a bagg of *dust* would be of as firm a consistence as that of *Marble* or *Adamant*'. Nevertheless he thought that it was the only explanation which 'with any shew of success hath yet appeared on the Philosophick Stage' [(1) 49].

Locke ignores both the Scholastic and the Cartesian explanations. He singles out for discussion one which was in fact proposed (independently) by Malebranche [Bk.6, sect.2,ch.9] and Jacob Bernoulli (1654-1705), the Swiss mathematician, with the aim of improving on Descartes while remaining within the bounds of his system. The idea here is that just as 'the pressure of the Particles of Air, may account for the cohesion of several parts of Matter, that are grosser than the Particles of air' so similarly 'the pressure of the Aether, or any subtiler Matter than the Air, may unite, and hold fast together the parts of a Particle of Air, as well as other Bodies' [II.xxiii.23]. Locke has two objections to this. His first is that it simply pushes the problem one step back. '[I]t leaves us in the dark, concerning the cohesion of the parts of the Corpuscles of the Aether it self' [II.xxiii.23; also 27].

His second is less obvious and concerns what he refers to as 'the Experiment of two polished Marbles' [II.xxiii.24]. It is a fact that if two flat pieces of polished marble are placed face to face it will be found difficult or impossible to pull the faces directly away from each other. It is, however, easy to separate them by sliding them one over the other. According to Lee, Locke had in mind Hobbes' reference to this fact 'in his Letter to K. *Charles* II. about a *vacuum*' [114]. Indeed perhaps Locke is referring to chapter 3 of Hobbes' 'Seven Philosophical Problems' dedicated to Charles II in 1662 [7.17-18]. But he could equally have known of the experiment from the descriptions given by Galileo in his *Dialogues concerning Two New Sciences* (1638), Malebranche in 1674 [Bk. 6, sect. 2, ch.9], or Boyle in 1661 [1.402-11, 4.295]. The experiment was interpreted differently by each of those who discuss it. According to Boyle it offered some support for the Cartesian explanation of cohesion [1.402, 411]. According to Locke it demonstrated the failure of the aether-pressure hypothesis. It showed that if the pressure of aether were all there were to cohesion then 'in every imaginary plain, intersecting any mass of Matter, there could be no more cohesion, than of two polished Surfaces, which will always, notwithstanding any imaginable pressure of a Fluid, easily slide one from another' [II.xxiii.24].

This objection of Locke's is quite fatal. But there are other less sophisticated ones which we might have expected him to make. He could have pointed out that according to this hypothesis it must be an increase of pressure that turns water to ice. But then water should contract on freezing and not expand as it does. He might also have pointed out that bodies do not fall apart in a vacuum.

The space-filling ability of body is not the only important thing about it which is a consequence of its solidity. The ability, an essential part of our idea of body, to communicate motion by impulse is another [II.xxiii.22]. Locke says twice in the *Essay* that the only way we can imagine bodies to move each other is by impulse on contact [II.viii.11, IV.x 19]. But he was later persuaded by 'the judicious Mr. Newton's incomparable book', *Principia*, that bodies are also able to act on each other at a distance by (gravitational) attraction [(5) 4.467-8; also 464-5]. He did not think, however, that this further possibility was essential to our idea of body in the way that the communication of motion by impulse was. He told Stillingfleet that he would take account of this change of view in the next edition of the *Essay*. There are some changes in the fourth edition in what he says about impulse, but it is not clear that they concede that bodies might act at a distance.

The ability to communicate motion by impulse is, then, more intelligible than any attractive power bodies may have. It is 'not beyond our Conception' [IV.iii.13]. Even so Locke says that we are 'in the dark' about it [II.xxiii.28, IV.iii.29, x.19]. What exactly is the problem Locke finds in the fact that colliding bodies move each other? This question is usually not asked explicitly. But Locke's commentators have implied an answer to it when they discuss what he says elsewhere about 'the obscure idea of active power' [*Gibson* 107; *Aaron* 184].

In a lengthy chapter on the idea of 'Power' [II.xxi] Locke distinguishes *active* from *passive* power, the power to make or produce change from the power to receive change. Where, he asks, do we get our idea of active power? Could we get it by seeing colliding billiard balls causing each other to move? Locke says we could not because when one ball 'by impulse sets another Ball in motion . . . it only communicates the motion it had received from another'. This, he says, 'gives us but a very obscure Idea of an active Power of moving in Body, whilst we observe it only to transfer, but not produce any motion' [II.xxi.4]. Why does such observation of colliding balls give us only an *obscure* idea of active power? It is often supposed that Locke has in mind that all we observe is *the bare fact that* one ball begins to move after another has approached and come into contact with it. We do not see *why* there should be produced any movement in the second ball. We have no clear insight into the active power of the first ball to produce that movement. If one takes what Locke says about active power in this way it would be easy to suppose that he has in effect provided an explanation of how we are 'in the dark' about the 'communication of motion by impulse'. On this understanding of it it would be easy to identify his view that we have only an obscure idea of active power with his difficulties about communication of motion. It would be easy to suppose that his difficulty is simply in seeing *why* one ball should move off after the other meets it.

Common though it is, this understanding of what Locke found problematic about colliding bodies moving each other, is mistaken. It has recently been made perfectly clear that it is based on a misreading of what he says about active power.[2] Locke in fact never suggests that the obscurity or inadequacy of our idea of active power can be traced to something opaque in the causal interaction between colliding balls. He never suggests that there is something there which we then fail to observe. What he does say is that colliding balls provide only an obscure idea of active power because they just do not have the active power to initiate movement in each other. We cannot get a clear idea of power to initiate movement from observing balls hitting each other simply because, as Locke explicitly says, *there is no production of movement in such cases*. What there is is only transfer of motion. Motion is *produced* when one thing *which is not moving* gets another to move. Active power is not a power merely to transfer motion. It is a power to produce it. So to get a clear idea of active power we need to look not to the impact of one object on another, but rather to the production of motion in our bodies by our minds.

It is obvious from this that having a clear, non-obscure idea of active power is, for Locke, simply not the same as understanding the communication of motion upon impulse. This conclusion can be reached from another direction. According to Locke we can't get a clear idea of active power from observation of colliding bodies, but we can get one from our own ability to initiate movement in our own bodies. Locke also says, however, that we don't find our own ability to initiate movement any more intelligible than that of material objects to communicate it. It follows then that even if we could get a clear idea of active power from observation of colliding bodies we still would not find the communication or transfer of motion intelligible. The fact that observation of colliding bodies provides us only with an obscure idea of active power is not the same as the fact that the transfer of motion in these collisions is unintelligible to us.

So just what it is that Locke finds incomprehensible about the way colliding bodies move each other is not to be explained in this way. Fortunately he says a little more about it. What happens in the 'communication of motion by impulse' as opposed to the initiation of motion as when we move our own bodies is that 'as much Motion is lost to one Body, as is got to the other'. But what is going on when motion is lost by one thing and gained by another? According to Locke, all we can imagine is happening is 'the passing of Motion out of one Body into another' [II.xxiii.28]. What he finds quite unclear apparently is the idea of motion transfer. What is it for motion to be transferred? What does 'transfer' mean in this context? Leibniz and Lee confirm that it is the idea of 'transfer' that is at the centre of Locke's worry. Leibniz objects to Locke that he finds a problem only because he has the too-literal idea that 'motion passes from subject to subject, and that the numerically same motion is taken across' [171]. Lee is more sympathetic to Locke in being puzzled himself by what happens 'when one body transfers the motion it has to another'. He makes clear that the puzzle has to do with the notion of transfer in special connexion with motion. For he asks, 'Is the Motion of one, for any instant of time, *separated* from both Bodies? That is impossible to conceive, how Motion should exist *separated* from all body. Do some *Effluvium's* pass from one to the other?'[115].

Locke's problem is something like this, then. Motion *can* be passed or transferred from one object to another. But is this like the transfer of a ball from one hand to another? A ball can exist independently of a hand which happens to hold it. Consequently one can talk in a straightforward way of the *same* ball being now in the one hand, now the other. It seems clear, however, that, as Lee says, motion cannot exist apart from any moving body. Is it then nonsense to speak of the motion of the second ball being the transferred earlier motion of the first? Leibniz is sure that it is. He says he is not surprised that Locke is puzzled since he seems 'to be entertaining something as inconceivable as an accident's passing from one subject to another'. For his part Leibniz can 'see no reason why we have to suppose such a thing' [224]. Is Leibniz right? Has Locke invented a pseudo-puzzle by thinking of 'motion transfer' literally as a transfer of some sort? It is not clear that Locke has. For one thing, we *do* speak of 'motion transfer'. Certainly, we cannot mean exactly the same thing as when we speak of the transfer of a ball from one hand to another. But if we say that motion is not literally but only metaphorically transferred we are allowing *some* basis for the figure of speech. Besides the fact that the truth of the matter is not entirely straightforward there is a further reason, one of a different sort, for not supposing that Leibniz is right and Locke wrong. This is that in fact he completely agrees with Locke on the crucial point that the communication of motion by impulse involves transfer of some sort. How can this be since Leibniz plainly thinks such transfer is actually impossible, not merely 'unimaginable' as does Locke? There is nothing inconsistent in his position, however. He *does* think, with Locke, that communication of motion involves transfer of some sort, and he does think that such transfer is impossible. These two things are quite consistent with each other and Leibniz accepts them both. But, accepting both, Leibniz also accepts their plain consequence that the communication of motion does not ever really take place [*Broad* 47-8].

We must now turn from body to mind, spirit, or soul. Our idea of the former is, we have seen, of 'a thing that is extended, figured, and capable of motion'. Our idea of the latter is of 'a substance that thinks, and has a power of exciting motion in body, by will or thought'. According to the Cartesian view, which again forms a background for Locke's, the one principal attribute of mind which forms its nature or essence is thought. In believing that thought is one essential element of mind Locke is therefore in partial agreement with Descartes for whom it is its 'one principal property'.

Locke's view that thinking is essential to minds is not the view that minds 'always think'. He means that they think from time to time, or are capable of and have the power of thinking. Early on in Book II there is an extended criticism of the 'Opinion, that the Soul always thinks, and that it has the actual Perception of Ideas in it self constantly, as long as it exists' [II.i.9]. This discussion is new to the final *Essay* and does not occur in the early drafts. Locke seems first to have been concerned about the point in about 1682 [(7) 121 f.]. He does not say who, if anyone, holds this opinion, but it is Descartes and his followers that he is in fact attacking.

There are many reasons for saying Locke has Descartes in mind here. For one thing, the 'opinion' *is* Cartesian, and Leibniz in his discussion of Locke explicitly says so [113]. For another, Locke's description of it as the opinion 'that actual thinking is as inseparable from the Soul, as actual Extension is from the body' [II.i.9] involves an allusion to another Cartesian doctrine. He says, furthermore, that 'the Men I have here to do with . . . liberally allow Life, without a thinking soul to all . . . Animals' [II.i.12]. These 'Men' are Cartesians. Descartes held that the difference between a living body and a dead one was like that between a moving machine and a stopped one. It had nothing to do with the presence of a soul. Animals, for Descartes, are like machines or automata and have no soul or minds, no sensation or thought [(3) 243-5]. A final reason is that, as we shall see, Locke's discussion of the matter echoes the objections which Antione Arnauld made to Descartes and Descartes' replies to them.

The Cartesian doctrine is that it is actually proceeding thinking, rather than the mere ability or capacity to think, that is of the essence of mind [(1) 2.141, 210]. Locke's, on the other hand, is that actually being engaged in thought is not essential to a mind or soul. For him, thinking does not stand to the soul like extension does to body. It is not ever-present and inseparable. It stands to it like *motion* does to body. Just as a material body may or may not be in actual movement, so mind may or may not be engaged in actual thought [II.i.10]. Contrary to the Cartesian view, we are not, says Locke, always thinking. At any rate, it is neither a self-evident truth nor one of experience that we are always thinking [II.i.10]. Descartes' view will seem very implausible unless we realise that by 'thought' he did not just mean deliberation or some strictly intellectual activity. He took thinking to include all forms of consciousness, anything that involved possession of a mind. 'By the word thought I understand all that of which we are conscious as operating in us. And that is why not alone understanding, willing, imagining, but also feeling, are here the same thing as thought' [(1) 1.222]. Locke refers to this wide use of 'thought' and appears to fall in with it himself.

In what he says Locke makes the basic assumption that we cannot think 'at any time waking or sleeping, without being sensible of it' [II.i.10]. It is 'altogether as intelligible to say, that a body is extended without parts, as that any thing thinks without being conscious of it, or perceiving, that it does so' [II.i.19]. This assumption marks a point of agreement between him and Descartes. He too holds that 'there can exist in us no thought of which, at the very moment that it is present in us, we are not conscious' [(1) 2.115; also 1.222, 2.13]. Both of them were criticised on the point. Writing against Locke, Sergeant pointed out that

> when a Man is quite absorpt in a serious Thought, or (as we say) in a *Brown Study*, his Mind is so *totally* taken up with the *Object* of his *present* Contemplation . . . that he can have no Thought, at that very Instant, of his own *Internal* Operation, or that he is *thinking*, or any thing like it. [(2) 121-2]

While Arnauld suggested to Descartes that there was nothing impossible about unconscious thought. We can see this, he maintained, if we consider children in the womb and 'innumerable similar instances' [*Descartes* (1) 2.93]. One might think, indeed, that Descartes' and Locke's idea that nothing thinks without being conscious or aware of it rests on a simple confusion. As Sergeant makes clear, it is one thing to be, whilst thinking of it, conscious of something. It is quite another reflexively to be conscious or thinking *of* that thinking or consciousness. Some writers on Descartes, however, suggest that the idea does not rest on mere confusion.[3]

The insistence that we cannot think without being conscious

of it makes it all the more initially difficult for Descartes to hold that we *are* always thinking. We do not seem to be conscious of thinking when asleep. For Descartes this would have to mean that we do not think then. If, on the other hand, it were allowed that thought need not be conscious of itself then the possibility would be open that we do always think, albeit unknowingly. These initial difficulties are brought out by Locke. Let us suppose (with Descartes) that the soul does always think. Let us also suppose (with Descartes and with Locke) that thinking must be self-aware. It then follows that when, as in sleep, we are not aware of thinking we will have to 'make the Soul think apart, what the Man is not conscious of '. This is to 'make the Soul and the Man two Persons' [II.i.12].

But though we are not conscious *now* that we thought in our sleep last night might it still not be that we did, and even were conscious at the time of doing so? This was Lee's reaction to Locke's objection [47] and would in fact have been Descartes'. 'Being conscious of our thoughts at the time when we are thinking them is not the same as remembering them afterwards'. He wrote in a letter to Arnauld who had raised exactly this problem about sleep, that 'we do not have any thoughts in sleep without being conscious of them at the moment they occur; though commonly we forget them immediately' [(3) 235].

Locke has a counter to this. He asks why it is that we cannot afterwards remember our thought during sleep. It looks as though he knew full well that the same question had already been put by Arnauld to Descartes himself [*Descartes* (1) 2.141]. For the reply which Locke constructs for those he is arguing against [II.i.15] has the appearance of being modelled on Descartes' own reply [(1) 2.210-11]. The thinking carried on by the soul during sleep fails to make on the brain any impression which is sufficiently strong for memory. Locke is not content with the reply. It again makes the thinking soul and the waking man 'two distinct Persons' [II.i.15].

Locke turns from the question of thinking and sleep to ask when the mind begins to think and about the possibility of prenatal thought. Descartes had been questioned by Arnauld about this very matter. His answer was clear. '[T]he mind begins to think at the same time as it is infused into the body of an infant, and is at the same time conscious of its own thought, though afterwards it does not remember that, because the specific forms of these thoughts do not live in the memory' [(1) 2.115]. Locke appears to be making a direct reply to this when he asks what the thought of such an infant which has not yet received any ideas from sensation consists in. 'Those who so confidently tell us, That the Soul always actually thinks, I would they would also tell us, what those Ideas are, that are in the Soul of a Child, before, or just at the union with the Body, before it hath received any by Sensation' [II.i.17]. As we might expect, Descartes himself was not blind to the problem raised here. According to the French writer Voltaire (1694-1778) he thought that the soul in the womb has metaphysical thoughts which it forgets afterwards [*Aaron* 90]. What Descartes says on this 'unexplored topic' in a letter contradicts this. His view does not mean, he says, 'that the mind of an infant meditates on metaphysics in its mother's womb . . . . [I]t seems most reasonable to think that a man newly united to an infant's body is wholly occupied in perceiving or feeling the ideas of pain, pleasure, heat, cold, and other similar ideas which arise from its union and intermingling with the body' [(3) 111].

We saw earlier that Locke rejects Descartes' view that extension is the whole essence of body. He agrees with him that it is at least part of its essence. But he sees other properties, such as solidity and the ability to communicate motion by impulse, as being essential also. In the case of mind too, Locke wants to add something to its Cartesian essence. Both hold that thought is of the essence of mind. According to Locke, however, there is more to it than that. Our idea of mind is not only of a substance that thinks but also of one that 'has a power of exciting Motion in a Body, by Will, or Thought' [II.xxiii.22]. What More said earlier on these topics is worth recording here. Locke could hardly agree with him that both bodies and minds are extended. But he would agree that essential to both is '*Activity* either connate or communicated', i.e. the power either to initiate movement or to communicate it [66].

The power mind has to move body is importantly different from the power bodies have of communicating motion to each other by impulse. Minds, which themselves do not move, can initiate movement in body. Bodies can only transfer or pass on movement which they already have. It is for this reason that, as we saw earlier, we can get from bodies only an *obscure* idea of active power. '[F]rom reflection on what passes in our selves', on the other hand, we can get a *clear* idea of active power, '[t]he Idea of the beginning of motion' [II.xxi.4]. We find from experience 'that barely by willing it, barely by a thought of the Mind, we can move the parts of our Bodies, which were before at rest' [II.xxi.4].

Locke finds neither of the two essential properties of mind, neither the power of thought nor the power to initiate movement, comprehensible. He does not, he says, know 'wherein Thinking consists' [IV.iii.6, vi.14]. We will come to this problem in a while. As for the power to initiate motion, this is no more comprehensible than the power of bodies to communicate it by impulse. 'Constant Experience makes us sensible of both of these, though our narrow Understandings can comprehend neither' [II.xxiii.28; also IV.vi.14, x.19]. Locke's problem is not simply that minds can do what bodies cannot. It is not simply that they can initiate motion, rather than merely pass it on. After all, minds are not bodies and it need be no surprise that they have abilities and powers which bodies lack. The problem is rather the converse of this. It is that though minds are unlike bodies they can nevertheless do something which bodies can. They can get something to move which was not moving before. Bodies can get other bodies to move because, as we have seen, they have a solidity which allows them to come into contact with and impel each other. But minds are not solid. How then can they get bodies to move? 'We cannot conceive how any thing but impulse of Body can move Body; and yet that is not a Reason sufficient to make us deny it possible, against the constant Experience, we have of it in our selves, in all our voluntary Motions, which are produced in us only by the free Action or Thought of our own Minds' [IV.x.19]. Locke's problem was shared by Boyle [4.416] and by Glanvill [(1) 21 f.]. More had felt it too. He too could not see how incorporeal spirit could move matter. '[I]t seems so subtile, that it will pass through, leaving no more footsteps of its being there, then the Lightening does in the Scabbard, though it may haply melt the Sword, because it there findes resistance' [80-1]. More felt, however, that so long as one could accept coherence and the communication of motion by impulse the ability of souls to move body had no *further* difficulty in it [82].

Locke had this problem because he accepts the Cartesian dualistic view that there are two kinds of created substance, minds and body. How can two entirely distinct substances of different kinds interact and affect each other? The problem was forced on Descartes' attention by the persistent questioning of his pupil Princess Elizabeth (1618-80), grand-daughter of James I of England [*Wilson* 205 ff.]. What worried Locke, Boyle, and More was how an immaterial spirit could get hold of and make contact with a material body. For Descartes the problem was sometimes more precise than this. If mind can initiate movement in body then motion is being created. But this contradicts his firmly held idea that there is in the universe a constant amount of motion. As a solution Descartes' followers such as Malebranche began to adopt the theory known as Occasionalism. According to this, mind does *not* actually move body, and interact with it. Boyle favoured this approach. The soul, he said, does not 'give any motion to the parts of the body, but only guide[s] or regulate[s] that which she finds in them already' [4.416].

The question how mind can affect body has, as the Cartesians recognised, a counterpart in how body can affect mind as in perception and sensation [*Wilson* 208 f.]. Locke was equally puzzled by it. He could see 'no conceivable connexion between any impulse of any sort of Body, and any perception of a Colour, or Smell, which we find in our Minds' and which are produced by them. We 'can reason no otherwise about them, than as effects . . . which perfectly surpass our Comprehensions' [IV.iii.28; also 13, 29, vi.14].

What Locke says about body and mind is said against the background of Descartes' dualism. Generally he accepts that, besides God, there are two distinct kinds of thing, material substance or body, and immaterial substance or mind or spirit [e.g. II.xxiii.3, 5, 32]. There is one notorious occasion, however, when he raises the possibility that matter might think and have some of the properties of spirit. From the ideas we have of matter and of thinking we cannot tell whether a material thing might not think. So far as our ideas go it may be possible for God to give 'to some systems of matter fitly disposed a power to think'. '[S]ince we know not wherein Thinking consists ... I see no contradiction in it, that the first eternal thinking Being should, if he pleased, give to certain Systems of created senseless matter, put together as he thinks fit, some degrees of sense, perception, and thought' [IV.iii.6]. Locke was closely questioned by Stillingfleet about this and much of their correspondence is taken up with the point [(5) 4.31 ff., 457 ff.]. He concedes to Stillingfleet that it is improbable that there is nothing immaterially spiritual about us and that we are simply thinking matter, but he still insists on the possibility [(5) 37].

The materialistic suggestion that matter might think would have been shocking in two ways to many in the seventeenth century. First, it would have seemed to count against immortality and life after death. A common line of reasoning was that thought and sensation could pertain only to something immaterial and that only something immaterial could be immortal. Locke refers to this 'usual ... proof ... of the immortality of the soul' in an entry in his Journal in 1682. 'Matter cannot thinke ergo the soule is immateriall, noe thing can naturally destroy an immateriall thing ergo the soule is naturally immortal' [(7) 121]. The first element of this thinking is endorsed by More when, in his *Immortality of the Soul*, he argues that '*Matter* from its own nature is uncapable of *Sense*' [120]. It is endorsed also by Richard Baxter (1615-91), a minister who wrote extensively on religion. In the appendix to his *Reasons of the Christian Religion* (1667) his first move in proving our immortality is to answer the suggestion that 'matter and motion may do all that which we ascribe to souls'. Glanvill outlines the whole line of thought together with the reaction of its opponents. From 'the nature of *sense*; the quickness of *imagination*; the *spirituality* of the *understanding*; the *freedom* of the *will* ... [people] infer, that the Soul is *immaterial*, and from *thence*, that it is *immortal*' [30-1]. Against this, however, some pretend 'that all things we *do*, are performed by *meer matter*, and *motion*, and consequently that there is no such thing as an *immaterial* being: and therefore that when our *bodies* are *dissolv'd*, the *man* is *lost*, and our *Souls* are *nothing*' [32]. We can see from what Glanvill says that Locke, in 1690, had not been the first to make the shocking suggestion that matter might think. Indeed materialism, with its supposed consequences for man's mortality and for atheism was a feature of the widespread revival of Epicurean atomism in the seventeenth century. The early atomist Hobbes was widely supposed to be an atheist and is a good example of 'a modern Sadduce' (as Glanvill [(2) 32] puts it) [3.380 f., 641 f., 4.60-1].

Glanvill's objection to the reasoning which suggests there can be no everlasting life is the same as Baxter's and More's. He accepts the inference that 'if there be nothing in us but *matter*, and the *results* of *motion*' [32] then that '*dismal* conclusion is *true*, and *certain*' But he denies its premiss. He argues that the more one studies nature the more one 'gains a clear sight of what *matter* can perform, and gets *more* and *stronger* Arguments . . . that it's *modifications*, and *changes* cannot amount to perception and *sense*' [33]. Locke is equally against the 'dismal conclusion' but he avoids it differently. In his view there is no connexion between matter and mortality. It seems to have been assumed at the time that immateriality automatically ensured immortality and that materiality necessitated mortality. Locke denies both of these assumptions. For him immortality was not a simple matter of enduring for ever. It meant always actually having thoughts and perceptions. So even if we are immaterial and cannot be destroyed it does not follow that we will enjoy an everlasting life of thought and perceptions. Even on earth, after all, the soul does not always think [(7) 121-3]. Similarly Locke did not accept that materialism would have to lead to our mortality. He adds to his suggestion that God might have disposed matter in such a way as to think that '[a]ll the great Ends of Morality and Religion, are well enough secured, without philosophical Proofs of the Soul's Immateriality; since it is evident, that he who made us first begin to subsist here, sensible intelligent Beings . . . can and will restore us to the like state of Sensibility in another World' [IV.iii.6]. If God can make matter think in this world and give us material 'souls' he can do so in the next. So even against the background of materialism immortality is a possibility. For Locke immortality neither follows from nor is inconsistent with materialism or with immaterialism. So even if we knew whether or not we are immaterial, immortality could not be *proved* either way. We have, however, the guarantee of revelation that we are in fact immortal [(5) 4.476].

The belief that it involved the heresy of human mortality would not have been the only reason why Locke's suggestion that matter might think would have been shocking to many in the seventeenth century. Particularly amongst its opponents there was an automatic tendency to associate the materialistic, mechanistic world-view of atomism with atheism. As a consequence its supporters in the Royal Society were keen to defend themselves and their investigations into the material world against this charge, and to distance themselves from Hobbesian irreligion. A large part of Sprat's *History of the Royal Society* is taken up with this defence. Similarly Glanvill's *Philosophia Pia* (1671) is an extended demonstration 'Of the Religious Temper, and Tendencies of the Experimental Philosophy which is protest by the Royal Society'. The mechanical philosophy does not lead to atheism, it was commonly suggested. For the more one studies nature the more one sees there must be a God. God can be found in his created works. Their order, beauty, and complexity amply testify to his existence:

> the more we understand of the *Laws* of *matter* and *motion*, the more shall we discern the *necessity* of a *wise* mind to *order* the blind, and insensible matter, and to *direct* the *original* motions; without the *conduct* of which, the *universe* could have been nothing but a mighty *Chaos*, and *mishapen* mass of everlasting *confusions*, and *disorders*. [*Glanvill* (2) 24]

But though Locke's suggestion of materialism may have been shocking to some, he too intended nothing atheistical by it. He is quick to point out to Stillingfleet that his suggestion that *we* might be purely material beings does not involve the denial of all spiritual immaterial beings. Indeed, as we have seen already in section 15, he thinks that the very assumption that we *are* merely thinking matter necessitates the existence of a spiritual God [(5) 4.36].

Notes

[1] *Animadversiones . . .Diogenis Laertii* (1649), 1.331-8.

[2] R.M. Mattern, 'Locke on Active Power and the Obscure Idea of Active Power from Bodies', *Studies in History and Philosophy of Science*, 11 (1980).

[3] R.McRae, 'Descartes' Definition of Thought', *Cartesian Studies*. ed. R.J. Butler (Blackwell, Oxford, 1972), pp.62f.

18 Conclusion

Many of the ideas and themes in the *Essay*, the stress on experiment and observation, the corpuscular theory of matter, the attacks on the Scholastics, the place given to reason in religion, belong not to Locke alone but also to his age. He was, nevertheless, a powerful and impressive spokesman and advocate for them. He brought them together, gave them a coherence, and presented them to a wider public with a vigorous voice.

Yet many of the early reactions to the *Essay* were critical. We have seen that those of Lee and of Stillingfleet were. The title of Lee's book, *Anti-Scepticism*, gives the clue that the object of attack was Locke's scepticism or supposed scepticism. To an extent Locke is a sceptic. He does put limits on our ability to know and understand. But he is hardly pessimistic about the human situation. He even wrote with the aim of defeating the despairing idea 'That either there is no such thing as Truth at all; or that Mankind hath no sufficient Means to attain a certain Knowledge of it' [I.i.2]. Nevertheless his polemic against innate ideas was taken to have dangerous consequences for religion and morality, the role he allotted to reason in religion was taken to imply an impersonal deism, and his suggestion that matter might think (despite his stress that '[a]ll the great Ends of Morality and Religion, are well enough secured') was pointed to with horror [*Yolton* (1)]. Berkeley, the first great British philosopher after Locke, reacted against what he saw as the sceptical and atheistical consequences of Locke's philosophy.

Despite the fact that on its publication in 1690 the *Essay* was giving voice to thoughts which were hardly novel (after all, the Royal Society received its charter in 1662) and despite the adverse nature of some of its early reception, the *Essay* became a popular classic in the eighteenth century. There were over two dozen editions of it then and, either in full or in the famous abridgement of it by Wynne, it became a set text for universities in England, Ireland, and Scotland. In fact it caught the imagination and set the tone for a whole era. Locke became (along with his friend and Royal Society colleague, Newton) one of the figureheads of the Age of Enlightenment.

In what way did Locke capture the imagination of an age? Gilbert Ryle reports how he and Bertrand Russell were once discussing why it was that Locke 'made a bigger difference to the whole intellectual climate of mankind than anyone had done since Aristotle' [147]. The suggestion that 'Locke invented common sense' met with Russell's immediate approval. 'By God, Ryle, I believe you are right. No one ever had Common Sense before John Locke – and no one but Englishmen have ever had it since'. In fact Ryle's suggestion was not as original as he implies. Much the same thing – though without Russell's chauvinistic gloss – had been said over two hundred years earlier in 1789 by Horace Walpole who, in a letter to the Countess of Ossory, commented that Locke was almost the first philosopher who introduced common sense into his writing. But, whoever made the suggestion first, there is a lot to be said for it.

As Ryle explains, what he has in mind in speaking of 'common sense' is a sober reasonableness in the adoption of beliefs, a due weighing of evidence, a lack of bias, prejudice, or partiality in one's attitudes and opinions, a proper caution, a thinking for oneself, and a refusal to accept anything on the basis of authority. This judiciousness pervades both the expression and the explicit doctrine of Locke's writings. Running through the *Essay* is an insistence that opinions are carefully to be weighed, considered and judged on their own merits, by each individual for himself, in independence of what others, particularly those in majority or authority, say. Expressing a sturdy, dogged, but polite individualism, he says:

> The Imputation of Novelty, is a terrible charge amongst those, who judge of Men's Heads, as they do of their Perukes, by the Fashion . . . . New Opinions are always suspected, and usually opposed, without any other Reason, but because they are not already common. But Truth, like Gold, is not the less so, for being newly brought out of the Mine. 'Tis Trial and Examination must give it price, and not any antick Fashion. [4]

True to this thought Locke urges his readers to 'use thy own Thoughts in reading' for it is 'not worth while to be concerned, what he says or thinks, who says or thinks only as he is directed by another' [7]. Men must be free and unfettered in their search for truth. We saw in section 3, in his rejection of innate ideas, and in section 4, in his strictures on the Scholastics, his desire to be free from authority and tradition in an unbiased search for the truth.

The rationalism of the Enlightenment era wears the colours of this sober common sense and of an individualism which is against tradition even though it developed in directions of which Locke might not have approved. He was, for example, quite clearly a Christian and believed in the Christian God, but there is no doubt that his chapters on faith and reason had a strong influence on the deistic movement towards a natural religion which came to maturity in the eighteenth century.

Locke contributed substantive content as well as tone, manner, and style to the Enlightenment. The eighteenth-century picture of the world and man's place in it derives at least in part from Locke. A famous passage in Paul D'Holbach's *System of Nature* (1770) says that the universe, 'that vast assemblage of everything that exists, presents us everywhere only with matter and motion: the whole offers to our contemplation nothing but an immense and uninterupted chain of causes and effects'. As for man, he is simply an element, a cog in this regularly ordered universe. 'He is the work of nature, he exists in nature, he is submitted to her laws . . . . For a being formed by nature, who is circumscribed by her laws, there exists nothing beyond the great whole of which he forms a part, of which he experiences the influence'.[1] This picture of the universe owes much to Newton whose theory of universal gravitation concerned itself with the whole universe. Save for one or two passages Locke tends not to look outwards beyond the earth [IV.iii.24]. His eyes are more often on things nearer at hand, on natural substances such as lead, gold, plants and the rest. But the mechanistic, matter-in-motion conception of the clock-like workings of the world is one which Locke did much to further.

The picture of man as part of nature derives from Locke too. Though he had been preceded by Hobbes in this, Locke treated man as a subject of investigation as much as anything else in nature. He follows, in his examination of the human understanding, just the plain, historical method of careful and honest observation which he recommends for the study of material substances. It has been pointed out how Locke's *Essay on the Human Understanding* was followed by a long series of others on the same theme: Berkeley's *Principles of Human Knowledge* (1710), Hume's *Treatise of Human Nature* (1739), Hartley's *Observations on Man* (1749), Condillac's *Treatise of Sensations* (1754), Helvétius' *On the Mind* (1758) and his *On Man* (1772).[2]

Locke's rejection of innate ideas, his suggestion that the mind begins as 'white Paper, void of all Characters, without any Ideas' [II.i.2] portrays man as coming into the world beholden to no prior authority, answerable only to reason and experience for his consequent opinions and beliefs. His account of 'all the materials of reason and knowledge' as combinations of simple ideas derived from sensation and reflection parallels the corpuscularian account of the properties of things. In detail this parallel may not hold, but the idea that the workings of the mind can be atomised, explained, traced and given a natural history along with any other part of the world is obviously significant. The framework of Locke's approach to the human mind influenced psychology and epistemology for a long time. Against the background of the idea that the mind is initially blank paper, people set themselves the problem of explaining how a mature person came to have the concepts, the understandings, the beliefs, the knowledge that he did. David Hartley (1705-57), Joseph Priestly (1733-1804), Francis Hutcheson (1694-1747), James Mill (1733-1836), and Étienne Condillac (1715-80) all approached this problem by analysing experience, after the manner of Locke, into elements and their combinations and associations.

These were not the only aspects of the *Essay* that made an impression on its readers. The shock-waves of his attack on Aristotelian logic and theory of demonstration, and his consequent stress on the need for experiment and observation can be traced over the years until they reach what has been called their 'ultimate fulfillment' in J.S. Mill's *System of Logic* (1843) [*Howell* 386].

Between the time of Locke's immediate influence and the present the course of philosophy and of thought in general has seen many revolutions and reactions. We should not expect to find Locke's effect on ourselves to be other than distant and indirect. Nevertheless his spirit has not disappeared and is not completely foreign to this century. Moreover a significant amount of philosophical discussion in the relatively recent past has centred round some of his particular doctrines. The *Essay* is not read simply as an historical document.

We have seen already how Gilbert Ryle and Bertrand Russell admired Locke's 'common sense' above all. Indeed Russell, whom many would say is the greatest philosopher of this century, with his cool, critical, and unsentimental intelligence, his intellectual free-enterprise, can often seem to be, if not Locke's spiritual son then his grandson, *via* the coolly detached Voltaire, who in fact learnt English in order to read Locke. It is clear, moreover, that the spirit of 'common sense' embodied in the desire to think for oneself, to weigh evidence and keep belief within its limits, and to put things to the test of reason and experience is thought by many people today to be of paramount value.

What of the influence of Locke's particular doctrines? Because of the account it gives of experience as the ultimate and sole source of the ideas and concepts which are the materials of knowledge, the *Essay* is often seen as a classical expression of the general philosophical viewpoint known as empiricism. In recent decades the influence of Ludwig Wittgenstein has stemmed the tide but many in this century have been and still are pleased to count themselves as empiricists. They have seen Locke's claim to be an 'Under-Labourer' [10] as symbolising the analysing and clarifying role they assign to philosophy. The most famous example of this is, perhaps, A.J. Ayer in *Language, Truth, and Logic* (1936), a book which itself is now a classic.

Apart from its reputation as a work of classical empiricism, and taking for granted that historians of philosophy and of thought in general attach great importance to it, the main interest in the *Essay* in recent years has been as a quarry out of which are mined theories, positions, or arguments, on a variety of isolated topics which happen for one reason or another to be of contemporary interest. Reference is frequently made in general philosophical discussion to the Lockean theory of substance, Locke's theory of representative perception, Locke's distinction between primary and secondary qualities, Locke's account of language and meaning, Locke's account of personal identity. From time to time this list would need amendment, for interests and fashions change. Merely in the past decade, for example, Locke's doctrine of real essence has been under scrutiny in connexion with a revival of interest in essentialism and natural kinds. Some of these topics have been played down or even ignored in this book. Others have been given a significance or meaning different from that which a less historical perspective might have given them. But this is as it should be, for, beginning from Locke's initial aim of tracing the origin, certainty, and extent of knowledge, I have tried to take the *Essay* as a whole and to explain it in its context.

Notes

[1] Quoted in G. Buchdahl, *The Image of Newton and Locke in the Age of Reason* (Sheed and Ward, London and New York, 1961), p.66.

[2] J.H. Randall, *The Makings of the Modern Mind* (Houghton Mifflin, Boston and New York, 1926), p.310.

Bibliography of Books and Articles referred to more than once

R.I. Aaron, *John Locke*, 3rd. edn. (Oxford University, Oxford, 1971).

M.R. Ayers, 'Mechanism, Superaddition, and the Proofs of God's Existence in Locke's *Essay*', *Philosophical Review*, 90 (1981).

Francis Bacon, *The Works*, 14 vols., ed. J.S. Spedding, R.L. Ellis, D.D. Heath (London, 1854-74: reprinted Frommann, Stuttgart, 1961-3).

J.F. Bennett, *Locke, Berkeley, Hume* (Clarendon Press, Oxford, 1971).

M.B. Bolton, 'Substances, Substrata, and Names of Substances in Locke's *Essay*', *Philosophical Review*, 85 (1976).

Robert Boyle, *The Works*, 6 vols., ed. T. Birch (London, 1772: reprinted Olms, Hildesheim, 1966).

C.D. Broad, *Leibniz: An Introduction* (Cambridge University, Cambridge, 1975).

Franco Burgersdijck, *Monito Logica or, an Abstract . . . of Logick*, trans. by a Gentleman [from the Latin of 1626] (London, 1697).

Richard Burthogge, *Philosophical Writings*, ed. M.W. Landes (Open Court, Chicago, 1921).

René Descartes, (1) *Philosophical Works*, 2 vols., trans, E.S. Haldane, G.R.T. Ross (Cambridge, 1911: reprinted Dover, New York, 1955).

(2) Passages trans. P.J. Crittenden in *Descartes: A Collection of Critical Essays*, ed. W. Doney (Macmillan, London, 1968).

(3) *Philosophical Letters*, trans. A. Kenny (Oxford University, Oxford, 1970).

H.R. Fox Bourne, *Life of John Locke*, 2 vols. (London, 1876: reprinted Scientia, Aalen, 1969).

James Gibson, *Locke's Theory of Knowledge* (Cambridge University, Cambridge, 1917)

Joseph Glanvill, (1) *The Vanity of Dogmatizing* (London, 1661: reprinted Harvester, Hove, Sussex, 1970, ed. S. Medcalf).

(2) *Philosophia Pia* (London, 1671: reprinted Olms, Hildesheim and New York, 1970).

Thomas Hobbes, *The English Works*, ed. W. Molesworth (London, 1840: reprinted Scientia, Aalen, 1962).

Robert Hooke, *Micrographia* (London, 1665: reprinted Dover, New York, 1961).

W.S. Howell, *Eighteenth-Century British Logic and Rhetoric* (Princeton University, Princeton, 1971).

R.F. Jones, *Ancients and Moderns*, etc., 2nd edn. (Washington University, St Louis, 1961).

W. H. Kenney, *John Locke and the Oxford Training in Logic and Metaphysics* (University Microfilms, Ann Arbor, 1960).

Henry Lee, *Anti-Scepticism* (London, 1702: reprinted Garland, New York and London, 1978).

G.W. Leibniz, *New Essays on Human Understanding*, trans. P. Remnant, J. Bennett (Cambridge University, London and New York, 1981).

John Locke, (1) Draft A of the *Essay* (1671), in *An Early Draft of Locke's Essay, together with Excerpts from his Journals*, ed. R.I. Aaron, J. Gibb (Clarendon, Oxford, 1936).

(2) Draft B of the *Essay* (1671), in *An Essay . . . by John Locke*, ed. B. Rand (Harvard University, Cambridge Mass., 1931).

(3) Draft C of the *Essay* (1685), in *Aaron*.

(4) Letters, extracts from Journals, and Commonplace Books, in *Life and Letters of John Locke* by Lord King (1884: reprinted Franklin, New York, 1972).

(5) *Works*, 10 vols. (London, 1823: reprinted Scientia, Aalen, 1963).

(6) *Correspondence*, 8 vols., ed. E.S. de Beer (Clarendon, Oxford, 1976-   ).

(7) Extracts from Journals, in (1) above.

James Lowde, *A Discourse concerning the Nature of Man* (London, 1694: reprinted Garland, New York and London, 1979).

H.G. Lyons, *The Royal Society, 1660-1940* (Cambridge University, Cambridge, 1944: reprinted Greenwood, New York, 1968).

J.L. Mackie, *Problems from Locke* (Clarendon, Oxford, 1976).

Nicholas Malebranche, *The Search after Truth*, trans. T.M. Lennon (Ohio State University, Columbus, 1980).

Henry More, *Philosophical Writings*, ed. F.I. Mackinnon (AMS, New York, 1969).

John Norris, *An Essay towards the Theory of the Ideal or Intelligible World* (London, 1701-4: reprinted Olms, Hidesheim and New York, 1974).

D.J. O'Connor, *John Locke* (Penguin, London, 1952: reprinted Dover, New York, 1967).

D.L. Perry, 'Locke on mixed modes, relations, and knowledge', *Journal of the History of Philosophy*, 5 (1967).

R.H. Popkin, *The History of Scepticism from Erasmus to Descartes* (Van Gorcum, Assen, 1964).

Henry Power, *Experimental Philosophy . . . in avouchment and illustration of the new atomical hypothesis* (London, 1664).

G. Ryle, *Collected Papers*, 2 vols. (Hutchinson, London, 1971).

John Sergeant, (1) *The Method to Science* (London, 1696).

(2) *Solid Philosophy Asserted . . . or, The Method to Science farther illustrated. With Reflexions on Mr Locke's Essay* (London, 1697).

Thomas Spencer, *The Art of Logick* (London, 1628: reprinted Scolar, Menston, 1970).

Thomas Sprat, *The History of the Royal-Society of London* (London, 1667: reprinted Routledge & Kegan Paul, London, 1959, ed. J.I. Cope, H.W. Jones).

H.G. Van Leeuwen, *The Problem of Certainty in English Thought: 1630-1690* (Nijhoff, The Hague, 1963).

John Webster, *Academiarum Examen* (London, 1653: reprinted in A.G. Debus, *Science and Education in the Seventeenth Century* (Macdonald, London and Elsevier, New York, 1970)).

P.P. Wiener, 'The Experimental Philosophy of Robert Boyle (1629-91)', *Philosophical Review*, 41 (1932).

M.D. Wilson, *Descartes* (Routledge & Kegan Paul, London, 1978).

J.W. Yolton, (1) *John Locke and the Way of Ideas* (Clarendon, Oxford, 1968).

(2) *Locke and the Compass of Human Understanding* (Cambridge University, Cambridge, 1970).

Suggestions for Further Reading

R.I. Aaron, *John Locke*, 3rd. edn. (Oxford University, Oxford, 1971). A first-rate work which serves as a possible source of material on details of Locke's thought. It includes an account of his political philosophy.

Robert Boyle, *Selected Philosophical Papers*, ed. M.A. Stewart (Manchester University, Manchester, 1979). This convenient selection from the work of Locke's friend and Royal Society colleague contains 'The Origin of Forms and Qualities', the classic account of Boyle's corpuscular philosophy and his objections to Scholasticism.

Maurice Cranston, *John Locke: A Biography* (Longmans, London and New York, 1957). The standard life of Locke. It shows him as a busy man of affairs, traveller, and correspondent.

James Gibson, *Locke's Theory of Knowledge and its Historical Relations* (Cambridge University, Cambridge, 1917, repr. 1960). A twentiety-century classic which, besides giving a detailed account of Locke's theory of knowledge, has separate chapters relating Locke to the Scholastics, Descartes, Leibniz, and English Philosophy.

Joseph Glanvill, *The Vanity of Dogmatizing* (1661: repr. Harvester, Hove, Sussex, 1970, ed. S. Medcalf). A readable work which gives a strong taste of the flavour of the 'new philosophy'.

R.F. Jones, *Ancients and Moderns*, 2nd. edn. (Washington University, St Louis, 1961). A fascinating and well-documented account of the intellectual cross-currents of the seventeenth century.

John Locke, *An Essay Concerning Human Understanding,* ed. P. Nidditch (Oxford University, Oxford, 1975).

John Locke, *Two Treatises of Government,* ed. P. Laslett (Cambridge University, Cambridge, 1960). The main source for Locke's political philosophy. This is the standard edition, with an important introduction.

Thomas Sprat, *The History of the Royal-Society of London* (1667: repr. Routledge & Kegan Paul, London, 1959, ed. J.I. Cope, H.W. Jones). The official history of the Royal Society written shortly after its foundation. It gives a very good idea of the aims, activities, and philosophy of the Society.

Ian Tipton (ed.), *Locke on Human Understanding: Selected Essays* (Oxford University, Oxford 1977). A good collection of recent articles, with suggestions for further study, on various aspects of Locke's theory of knowledge.

Index

Bold-faced page numbers following a name indicate biographical material